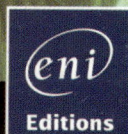

Microsoft® Office XP
WORD 2002
Expert

Copyright - Editions ENI - September 2001
ISBN: 2-7460-1405-X
Original edition: 2-7460-1396-7

Editions ENI

BP 32125
44021 NANTES Cedex 1

Tél. 02.51.80.15.15
Fax 02.51.80.15.16

e-mail : editions@ediENI.COM
http://www.editions-eni.com

Collection directed by Corinne HERVO
English edition by Adrienne TOMMY

MOUS
Word 2002 Expert

INTRODUCTION

DOCUMENT CONTENTS AND PRESENTATION

LONG DOCUMENTS

MAIL MERGE

OTHER ADVANCED FUNCTIONS

SUMMARY EXERCISES

This logo is your guarantee that you are using a Microsoft®-approved preparation guide for the Microsoft® Office User Specialist Word 2002 Expert exam.

This complete preparation guide provides you with the theory that explains all the features tested in the exam and practical exercises that you can work through, to find out how much you really know. When you can work through all these exercises, successfully and easily, you are ready to take the MOUS exam. At the end of the book, there is a list of all the Word 2002 Expert exam objectives and the lesson number and exercise that relate to each objective.

For further information on the titles in the MOUS collection, visit the ENI Publishing Web site, at www.eni-publishing.com; click the **Catalogue** link and then click the **MOUS** link in the list of ENI collections.

What is the MOUS certification ?

The MOUS (Microsoft Office User Specialist) exam gives you the opportunity to obtain a meaningful certification, recognised by Microsoft®, for the Office applications: Word, Excel, Access, PowerPoint, and Outlook. This certification guarantees your level of skill in working with these applications. It can provide a boost to your career ambitions, as it proves that you can use effectively all the features of the Microsoft Office applications and thus offer a high productivity level to your employer. In addition, it is a certain plus when job-seeking: more and more companies require employment candidates to be MOUS certificate holders.

What are the applications concerned?

You can gain MOUS certification in Word 97 and Excel 97 as well as the Office 2000 and Office XP applications: Word, Excel, Access, Powerpoint and Outlook. For Word 97 and Excel 97, only one level exists. However, there are two levels available for Word 2000, Excel 2000, Word 2002 and Excel 2002, consisting of a Core level, for basic skills and an advanced Expert level. If you obtain the Expert level for Word and Excel as well as MOUS certification in PowerPoint, Access and Outlook (Office 2000 or XP), you are certified as a Master.

How do you apply to sit the exams?

To enrol for the exams, you should contact one of the Microsoft Authorized Testing Centers (or ATC). A list of these centres is available online at this address: http://www.mous.net. There is also http://www.mous.edexcel.org.uk specifically for the UK. Make sure you know the version of the Office application for which you wish to obtain the certificate (is it the 97, 2000 or 2002 version?).

There is an enrolment fee for each exam.

On the day of the exam, you should carry some form of identification and, if you have already sat a MOUS exam, your ID number.

What happens during the MOUS exam?

During the exam, you will have your own computer, on which you must perform a series of set tasks in the application concerned. Each action required to perform each task is tested, to ensure that you have done exactly what you were asked to do.

You are allowed no notes, books, pencils or calculators during the exam. You can consult the application help, but you should be careful not to exceed the exam's time limit.

Each exam is timed; it lasts in general between 45 minutes and one hour.

How do you pass the exam?

You must carry out a certain percentage of the required tasks correctly, within the allocated time. This percentage varies depending on the exam.

You will be told your result as soon as you have finished your exam. These results are confidential (the data are coded) and are only made known to the candidate and to Microsoft.

What happens then?

You will receive a Microsoft-approved exam certificate, proving that you hold the specified MOUS (Microsoft Office User Specialist) level.

How this book works

This book is the ideal companion to an effective preparation of the **MOUS Word 2002 Expert** exam. It is divided into several sections, each containing one or more **chapters**. Each section deals with a specific topic: document contents and presentation (text, styles and templates, tables, charts, objects), long documents (sections, notes, bookmarks, outlines, tables of contents, indexes, tables of figures, tables of authorities and master documents), forms, mail merges, macros, managing toolbars and smart tags, workgroups (such as managing several versions of a document and tracking changes) and Web pages. Each chapter is independent from the others. You can tailor the training to suit you: if you already know how to format paragraphs, for example, you can skip this lesson and go straight to the practice exercise for that chapter, then if you feel you need some extra theory, you can look back at the relevant points in the lesson. You can also study the lessons and/or work through the exercises in any order you wish.

At the end of the book, there is an **index** to help you find the explanations for any action, whenever you need them.

From theory...

Each chapter starts with a **lesson** on the theme in question and the lesson is made up of a variable amount of numbered topics. The lesson should supply you with all the theoretical information necessary to acquire that particular skill. Example screens to illustrate the point discussed enhance the lesson and you will also find tips, tricks and remarks to complement the explanations provided.

...To practice

Test your knowledge by working through the **practice exercise** at the end of each chapter: each numbered heading corresponds to an exercise question. A solution to the exercise follows. These exercises are done using the documents on the CD-ROM accompanying the book, that you install on your own computer (to see how, refer to the INSTALLING THE CD-ROM instructions). In addition to the chapter exercises, four **summary exercises** dealing with each of the section themes are included at the end of the book. The solutions to these exercises appear as documents on the CD-ROM.

All you need to succeed!

When you can complete all the practice exercises without any hesitation or problems, you are ready to sit the MOUS exam. In the table of contents for each chapter, the topics corresponding to a specific exam objective are marked with this symbol: 🔲. At the back of the book, you can also see **the official list of the Word 2002 Expert exam objectives** and for each of these objectives the corresponding lesson and exercise number.

Free online training

Editions ENI have developed a series of practice tests for the MOUS exams. These tests are free and can be found on the www.moustest.com site. These tests take place online, within the application in question, just like in the official exam. To use this, you need an Internet connection on your computer, the application (e.g. Word 2000) and Internet Explorer 5.0 or later. At the end of the test, you can see your results in detail.

INTRODUCTION
How this book works

The layout of this book

This book is laid out in a specific way with special typefaces and symbols so you can find all the information you need quickly and easily:

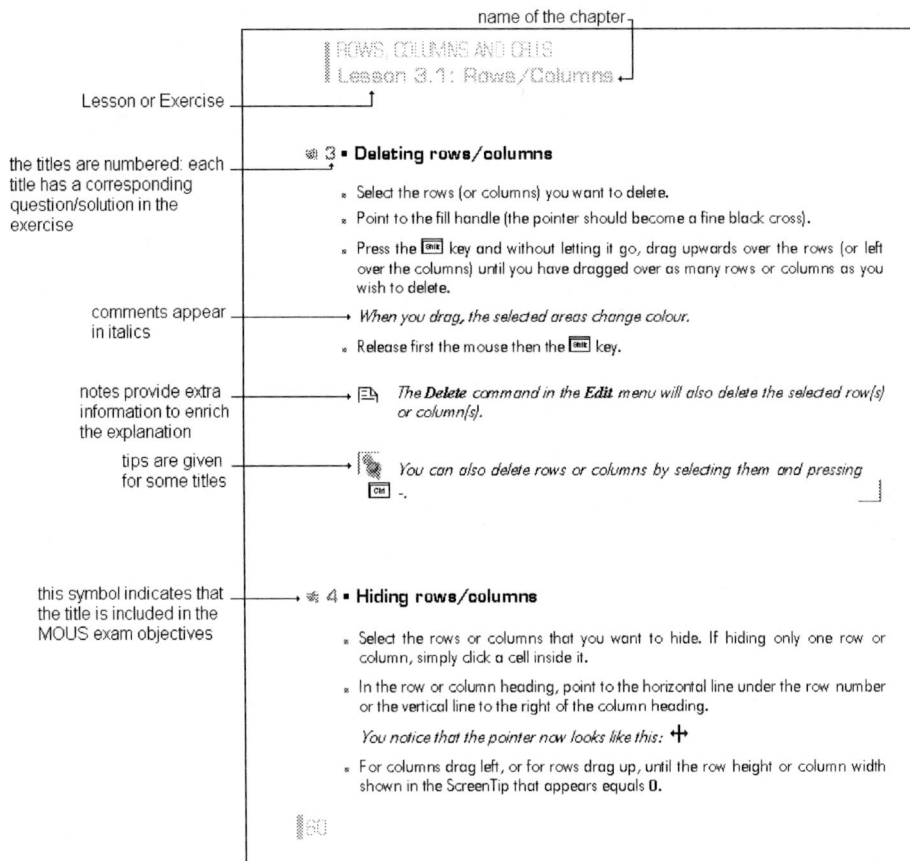

name of the chapter

ROWS, COLUMNS AND CELLS
Lesson 3.1: Rows/Columns

Lesson or Exercise

the titles are numbered: each title has a corresponding question/solution in the exercise

☜ 3 ▪ **Deleting rows/columns**

▪ Select the rows (or columns) you want to delete.

▪ Point to the fill handle (the pointer should become a fine black cross).

▪ Press the ⌧ key and without letting it go, drag upwards over the rows (or left over the columns) until you have dragged over as many rows or columns as you wish to delete.

comments appear in italics

When you drag, the selected areas change colour.

▪ Release first the mouse then the ⌧ key.

notes provide extra information to enrich the explanation

📭 *The **Delete** command in the **Edit** menu will also delete the selected row(s) or column(s).*

tips are given for some titles

✎ *You can also delete rows or columns by selecting them and pressing* ⌧ -.

this symbol indicates that the title is included in the MOUS exam objectives

☜ 4 ▪ **Hiding rows/columns**

▪ Select the rows or columns that you want to hide. If hiding only one row or column, simply click a cell inside it.

▪ In the row or column heading, point to the horizontal line under the row number or the vertical line to the right of the column heading.

You notice that the pointer now looks like this: ✛

▪ For columns drag left, or for rows drag up, until the row height or column width shown in the ScreenTip that appears equals 0.

You can tell whether an action should be performed with the mouse, the keyboard or with the menu options by referring to the symbol that introduces each action: 🖱, ⬡ and 📄.

Installing the **CD-ROM**

The CD-ROM provided contains the documents used to work through the practice and summary exercises and the summary exercise solutions. When you follow the installation procedure set out below, a folder called MOUS Word 2002 Expert is created on your hard disk and the CD-ROM documents are decompressed and copied into the created folder. The CD-ROM also contains two templates which you should copy into the Word Templates folder.

※ Put the CD-ROM into the CD-ROM drive of your computer.

※ Right-click the **Start** button and take the **Explore** option.

※ In the left pane of the Explorer window, scroll through the list until the CD-ROM drive icon appears. Click this icon.

The contents of the CD-ROM appear in the right pane of the Explorer window. The documents used for the practice and summary exercises are compressed in the MOUS Word 2002 Expert.exe file, although they also exist in standard form in the Practice Exercises and Summary folders. The templates are in the MOUS Templates folder.

※ Double-click the icon of the **MOUS Word 2002 Expert** folder in the right pane of the Explorer window.

*The **MOUS Word 2002 Expert** dialog box appears.*

※ Click **Next.**

The installation application offers to create a folder called MOUS Word 2002 Expert.

※ Modify the proposed folder name if you wish then click **Next**. If several people are going to be doing the practice exercises on the same computer, you should modify the folder name so each person is working on their own copy of the folder.

※ Click **Yes** to confirm creating the **MOUS Word 2002 Expert** folder.

The installation application decompresses the documents then copies them into the created folder.

* Click **Finish** when the copying process is finished.

  You must now copy the templates into the templates folder used by Word. Depending on the version of Windows you are using, the default file path to the Templates folder can vary. For Windows 98 and Me, the path is generally C:\Windows\Application Data\Microsoft\Templates, and for Windows 2000 Professional the path is usually C:\Documents and Settings\user_name\ Application Data\Microsoft\Templates.

* If you are working in Windows 2000 Professional, use the **Tools - Options** command in the Windows Explorer, click the **View** tab and activate the **Show hidden files and folders** option, which ensures that the entire hierarchy of files on your computer appears (this is not the case by default in Windows 2000).

* Click the folder called **MOUS Templates** in the right pane of the Explorer.

* Open the **Edit** menu then click the **Copy** option to copy the folder into the Windows clipboard.

* If necessary, scroll through the contents of the left pane of the window until you can see the **Windows** folder or **Documents and Settings**, depending on your version of Windows. Click the plus (+) sign to the left of the folder to see a list of the folders it contains.

  The + sign becomes a - sign.

* Click the + sign to the left of each subfolder, following the stated file path until you reach the **Templates** folder.

  By default, the templates are stored in this folder.

* Use the **Edit - Paste** command to copy the contents of the clipboard into the **Templates** folder.

* Some of the files copied directly from the CD-ROM are read-only files, which means they cannot be modified. As you need to work on these files for some of the exercises, you will need to remedy this problem: select the templates using `Ctrl`-clicks (for nonadjacent files) and/or `Shift`-clicks for adjacent files then right-click the selection and take the **Properties** option. Deactivate the **Read only** option and confirm with **OK**.

- If you are using Windows 2000 Professional, you can, if you wish, deactivate the **Show hidden files and folders** option in **Tools - Options - View** tab of the Windows Explorer.

- When the copy is finished, click the ☒ button on the **Explorer** window to close it.

You can now put away the CD-ROM and start working on your MOUS exam preparation.

DOCUMENT CONTENTS AND PRESENTATION
Lesson 1.1: Text

1 ▪ Preventing breaks within/between paragraphs

Page breaks or column breaks are often undesirable in the middle of a paragraph, or between complementary paragraphs.

▪ If you want to avoid a page/column break within a certain paragraph, select that paragraph. If you want to avoid a break between two paragraphs, click the first paragraph. If you want to avoid breaks between several paragraphs, select all the paragraphs except the last.

▪ **Format - Paragraph** or double-click one of the four indentation markers

▪ Activate the **Line and Page Breaks** tab.

▪ To avoid a page/column break within a paragraph, tick the **Keep lines together** option; to avoid a page/column break between paragraphs, tick the **Keep with next** option.

▪ Tick the **Widow/Orphan control** option to prevent the last line of a paragraph appearing at the top of a page (widowed) or the first line of a paragraph appearing alone at the bottom of a page (orphaned).

▪ Click **OK**.

🖿2 ▪ Inserting a manual page break

▪ Position the insertion point at the beginning of the line that will follow the page break.

▪ Press the Ctrl ↵ keys.

> vegetation· is· rich.· Forests· (pine,· palm,· cypress,· mangrove)· cover· 35%· of· the· state's· surface· area.· The· capital· of· Florida· is· Tallahassee.· The· main· towns· are· Jacksonville,· Miami·and·Tampa.·The·area·of·the·state·is·58°664°sq°miles·(151°940°km2).¶
>
> ···Page Break···
>
> **Economy**¶
> ──
> The· economy· in· Florida· has· boomed· during· the· 20ᵗʰ°century.· Today,· the· economy· is· diverse.· The· main· mineral· resources· are· phosphates,· oil· and· natural· gas.· Agriculture·

In Normal view, a dotted line representing the page break appears on the screen (provided the non-printing characters are visible). Word reminds you that there is a page break at that point in the text.

📄 *To remove a manual page break of this kind, place the insertion point on the dotted line and press the Del key.*

*The Ctrl ↵ shortcut performs the same action as the **Page Break** option in the **Insert - Break** menu.*

🖿3 ▪ Inserting a line break

Using a line break lets you start a new line without creating a new paragraph.

▪ Place the insertion point at the end of the line concerned.

▪ Press the Shift ↵ keys.

The insertion point moves onto the next line without starting a new paragraph.

⁂ If you wish, activate the display of non-printing characters (click the ¶ tool button) to see how Word represents a line break:

> Florida·is·the·27ᵗʰ·American·state.·↵
> It·is·situated·in·the·south·east·of·the·United·States,·with·
> the·Atlantic·off·the·east·coast·and·the·Gulf·of·Mexico·to·
> the·west.¶

The first line of this text finishes with a line break.

4 ▪ Sorting paragraphs

⁂ Select the paragraphs you want to sort.

⁂ **Table - Sort**

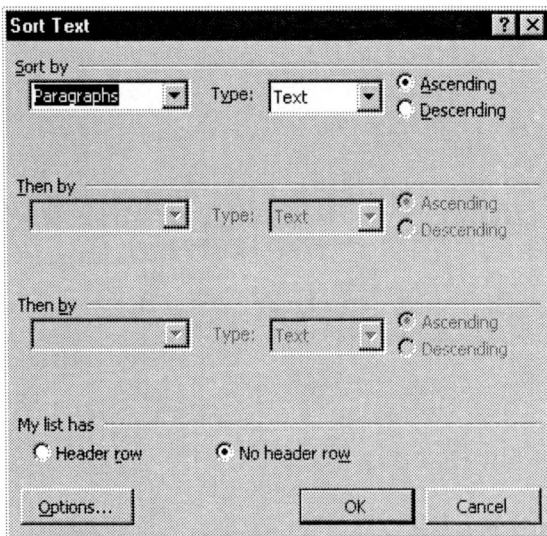

⁂ In the first list in the **Sort by** frame, leave the **Paragraphs** option active to sort by the first word of each paragraph.

If the first words in the selected paragraph are identical, Word will sort by the second word and so on.

* In the **Type** drop-down list, choose the kind of data you want to sort: **Text**, **Number** or **Date** (provided that the data includes at least the day and month or the month and year).

* Indicate whether you want to sort in **Ascending** or **Descending** order.

* If the first paragraph contains headers and is not to be sorted, activate the **Header row** option in the **My list has** frame.

* Click **OK**.

DOCUMENT CONTENTS AND PRESENTATION
Exercise 1.1: Text

Below, you can see **Practice Exercise** 1.1. This exercise is made up of 4 steps. If you do not know how to do one of the steps, go back to the title that corresponds to that particular lesson. When you have finished, you can check your work by reading the **Solution** that follows.

All the parts of this exercise are likely to be tested on the MOUS exam.

☞ Practice Exercise 1.1

To work on practice exercise 1.1, open the **1-1 Florida Intro.doc** document, located in the **MOUS Word 2002 Expert** folder.

1. On page 1 of this document, prevent a page break occurring in the middle of the paragraph which begins with the text **Florida only began to flourish....**

2. Insert a page break before the **Geography** title and another before the **Economy** title.

3. Insert a line break before the text **It is situated in the south east** that appears in the paragraph directly beneath the "FLORIDA" title, on the first page.

4. Sort in ascending order the paragraphs starting with dates in the section of the document entitled **History**.
   Finish by closing the **1-1 Intro Florida.doc** document, saving the changes you have made.

If you would like to practise these features more, on another document, you should work through Summary Exercise 1, on DOCUMENT CONTENTS AND PRESENTATION. You will find the summary exercises at the end of the book.

It is often possible to perform a task in several different ways, but here, only the easiest solution is presented. You can go back to the corresponding lesson if you want to see other techniques you could use.

Solution to Exercise 1.1

1. To prevent a page break occurring in the middle of the paragraph which begins with the text "Florida only began to flourish...", start by clicking this paragraph to place the insertion point in it.
   Use the **Format - Paragraph** command then click the **Line and Page Breaks** tab. Click the **Keep lines together** check box and click **OK**.

2. To insert a page break before the "Geography" section, place the insertion point before the letter **G** in the word **Geography** then press the [Ctrl][↵] keys.

   To insert a page break before the "Economy" section, place the insertion point before the letter **E** in the word **Economy** then press the [Ctrl][↵] keys.

3. To insert a line break before the text "It is situated in the south east" that appears in the paragraph directly beneath the main "FLORIDA" title, place the insertion point in front of before the letter **I** (in **It**) then press the [Shift][↵] keys.

4. To sort in ascending order the paragraphs in the "History" section starting with dates, select the text from the paragraph that begins with **1763** to the paragraph that begins with **1868**.
   Use the **Table - Sort** command. In the first list box in the **Sort by** frame, make sure the **Paragraphs** option is active.
   In the **Type** list, make sure the **Text** option is active and if necessary, choose **Ascending** order by clicking this option.

Check that the **No header row** option is active, under **My list has**, then click **OK**.

Close the document with the **File - Close** command and click **Yes** on the message that appears, to save your changes.

DOCUMENT CONTENTS AND PRESENTATION
Lesson 1.2: Styles and templates

▦1 ▪ Creating a style

A style contains character, paragraph and/or table formatting properties. Creating a style saves these presentations so you can apply them easily at another time. Styles are saved with the document or in a template.

Creating a style based on existing formatting

With this technique, you can only create paragraph styles, not character or table styles.

* If necessary, open the document or template to be used.

* If it is not already done, apply all the formatting you want to include in the style.

* Place the insertion point in the formatted paragraph.

* Click the name of the active style in the **Style** list box on the **Formatting** toolbar.

* Type the name of the new style and press ⏎ to confirm.

*In the example above, the new style has been called **Tour** and is applied immediately to the current paragraph.*

📄 *You can also use the **Styles and Formatting** task pane to create a style based on existing formatting. Open the task pane, point to the formatting type, click the* ⬛ *button and choose **Modify**. Enter a **Name** for the style in the corresponding text box and click **OK**. The formatting is saved as a style and this style is applied to all the paragraphs in the document (or template) which have that type of formatting.*

Creating a style without existing formatting

» **Format - Styles and Formatting** or ⬛

The ***Styles and Formatting*** task pane opens.

» Click the **New Style** button.

» Enter a **Name** for the style in the corresponding text box.

» If the style concerns a **Character**, **Table** or **List** presentation (cf. next section), choose that option in the **Style type** list. The default **Style type** is **Paragraph**.

» If you wish, choose a style on which to base your new style in the **Style based on** list.

» If you are creating a **Paragraph** style, you may want to open the **Style for following paragraph** list and choose the style that will be applied automatically to the next paragraph. When you press ⏎ at the end of a paragraph to which the new style is applied, Word will give the style you chose in the list to the next new paragraph.

» Using the tools and lists in the **Formatting** frame or the options available through the **Format** button, modify the formatting attributes for the style. If you are creating a **Table** style, you should specify, before changing the formatting, which part of the table this style should be applied to (use the **Apply formatting to** list for this).

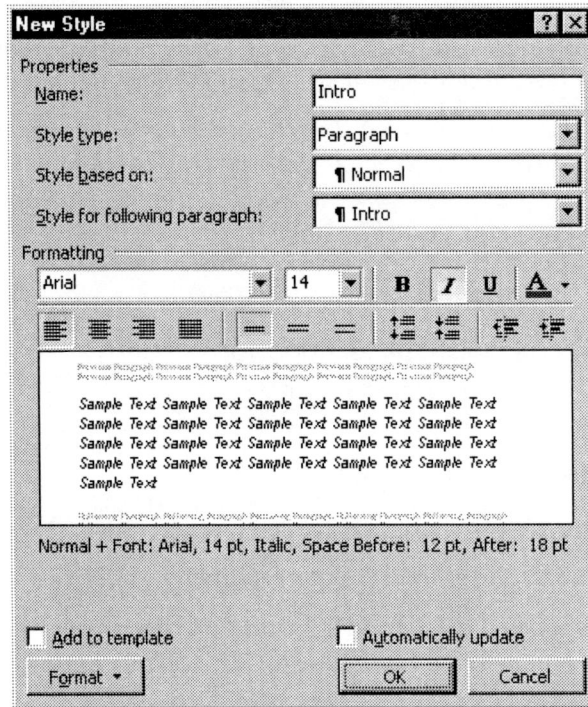

* Tick the **Add to template** option if you are not working in a template but you want to add the style to the template associated with the active document.

* Tick the **Automatically update** option if you want to carry over into the style itself any changes made to a paragraph presented with that style.

   This option is not available for character or table styles.

* Click **OK**.

   *The name of the style now appears in the **Styles and Formatting** task pane. The names of paragraph styles are followed by a ¶ symbol, the names of character styles by a ª and table styles by a ⊞ symbol.*

Creating a list style

A list style is a style that contains various levels of formatting; when you apply a style of this type, the formatting applied to each paragraph depends on its level. The level of a paragraph is determined by the value of the left indent: as a rule the more the paragraph is indented, the lower its level (for example, if a left indent of 1.5 cm is identified with level 2, the list style will apply level 2 formatting to all the selected paragraphs with an indent of 1.5 cm).

▪ If necessary, open the document or template concerned.

▪ **Format - Styles and formatting** or

▪ Click the **New Style** button on the **Styles and Formatting** task pane.

▪ Enter the **Name** for the new style in the dialog box which appears.

▪ Choose the **List** option in the **Style type** list.

▪ Define the formatting for each level in the following way:

- Select the level concerned in the **Apply formatting to** list.

- Select a new starting number from the **Start at** list (for paragraphs of this level to be numbered independently of the previous level paragraphs).

- Define the formats to apply to paragraphs of this level: use the tool buttons in the lower part of the dialog box and access further options by clicking the **Format** button.

* Tick the **Add to template** check box if you are not working in the template but you want to add the list style to the template on which the current document is based.

* Click **OK**.

*The name of the new style appears in the **Styles and Formatting** task pane.*

2 ▪ Applying a style

There are two ways of applying to text or a table the formatting attributes saved in a style.

First method

* To apply a character style, select the text concerned; to apply a paragraph style, select the paragraphs or click the paragraph concerned; to apply a table style, click the table concerned; to apply a list style, select the paragraphs concerned.

▪ Open the **Style** list on the **Formatting** toolbar.

```
Intro                    ▼
  Clear Formatting
  Blue characters        a
  Day                    ¶
  Heading 1              ¶
  Heading 2              ¶
  Heading 3              ¶
  Intro                  ¶
  Normal                 ¶
    Paragraph            ¶
  Tour                   ¶
```

▪ Click the name of the style you wish to apply.

The formatting contained in the style is applied immediately to the selection.

Second method

▪ To apply a character style, select the text concerned; to apply a paragraph style, select the paragraphs or click the paragraph concerned; to apply a table style, click the table concerned; to apply a list style, select the paragraphs concerned.

▪ If it is hidden, show the **Styles and Formatting** task pane by clicking the 🄰 tool button on the **Formatting** toolbar.

▪ Click the name of the style you want to apply.

If the insertion point is in a blank paragraph and you click the name of a table style, Word offers to insert a table by opening the ***Insert Table*** *dialog box.*

When you point to a style name in the task pane, a description appears in a ScreenTip.

If a keyboard shortcut is associated with that style, you can use that shortcut to apply the style to the selected character(s), paragraph(s) or table(s).

Whatever the method you use, using a style never limits the formatting applied to a paragraph. You can always add other types of formatting to those characters or paragraphs.

*To cancel the use of a style, open the **Style** list on the **Formatting** toolbar or show the **Styles and Formatting** task pane. Click **Clear Formatting** to cancel a character or paragraph style or **Table Grid** to cancel a table style.*

3 ▪ Managing styles

Modifying a style

The mouse solution can only be used to modify character and paragraph styles.

▪ If the modifications are only to affect the active document, make them in the document. If you want the modifications to carry over into any new document made from the template, make the changes in the template.

▪ Make the formatting changes on text that already uses the style you wish to modify (character or paragraph styles only).

▪ If it is hidden, show the **Styles and Formatting** task pane by clicking the tool button on the **Formatting** toolbar.

▪ In the **Pick formatting to apply** list, point to the style you want to modify, click the button and choose **Update to Match Selection**.

The changes made to the style are carried over to all the characters or paragraphs to which the style has previously been applied.

■ Activate the document or template containing the style you wish to modify.

■ If it is hidden, show the **Styles and Formatting** task pane by clicking the tool button on the **Formatting** toolbar.

■ In the **Pick formatting to apply** list, point to the style you want to modify, click the button and choose **Modify**.

■ Using the tools in the **Formatting** frame or the options accessed with the **Format** button, modify the formatting options for the style.

■ Tick the **Add to template** option if you are not working in a template but you want to add the style to the template associated with the active document.

■ Click **OK**.

The changes made to the style are carried over to all the characters or paragraphs to which the style has previously been applied.

*To modify the standard presentation of characters, you should modify the style called **Normal**.*

Deleting a style

■ Activate the document or template containing the style you wish to delete.

■ If it is hidden, show the **Styles and Formatting** task pane by clicking the tool button on the **Formatting** toolbar.

■ In the **Pick formatting to apply** list, point to the style you want to modify, click the button and choose **Delete**.

■ Confirm deleting the style by clicking the **Yes** button.

If you delete a style in a template, the style is not deleted in existing documents based on that template and vice versa.

Word's own predefined styles such as **Normal, Heading 1, Heading 2** and so on (which are in the Normal.dot template) cannot be deleted.

Printing the list of styles

* Open the template or document containing the styles you want to print.

* **File - Print** or Ctrl **P**

* Open the **Print what** list and choose to print the **Styles**.

* Click **OK**.

The styles are printed in alphabetical order, along with a description of their characteristics.

To see the styles in a document, activate **Normal** view, use the **Tools - Options** command and click the **View** tab. Enter a width (1.5 cm for example) in the **Style width area** box and enter: the names of the styles used in each paragraph appear on the left side of the screen.

4 ▪ Creating a document template

A template is a document in which you can save presentation styles and/or text in order to reuse them. Any new document is based on a template, the default template being Normal.dot.

You can create your own template from scratch, adding styles, text and so on, or you can create a template from a document already containing the required styles and/or texts.

Creating a template based on an existing template

⁂ If it is not on the screen, show the **New Document** task pane with the **File - New** command.

⁂ Click the **General Templates** link in the **New from template** section.

Do not use the 🗋 *tool button on the **Standard** toolbar or the* ⌃Ctrl *N shortcut or you will not be able to access the **Templates** dialog box.*

⁂ Click the **Template** option under **Create New**.

⁂ To base your new template on the Normal.dot template, make sure the **Blank Document** icon is selected on the **General** page. Otherwise, activate the appropriate tab and click the template on which you wish to base the new one.

⁂ Click **OK**.

The title bar reminds you that you are creating a new template.

⁂ Set out the styles, text and layout for your new template.

DOCUMENT CONTENTS AND PRESENTATION
Lesson 1.2: Styles and templates

※ **File - Save** or ⊟ or Ctrl **S**

*Word offers to save the template in the **Templates** folder. The **General** page in the **Templates** dialog box shows the templates that exist in this folder.*

※ In the **File name** box, give the name of the template.

Templates have a .dot file extension.

※ Click the **Save** button.

📄 *Templates that you create are stored by default in the **Templates** folder. The default file path for this folder changes, depending on the version of Windows you are using. Under Windows 98 and Me, the file path is C:\Windows\Application Data\Microsoft\Templates and under Windows 2000 Professional, the file path is C:\Documents and Settings\user name\Application Data\Microsoft\Templates.*

*To save templates in another folder than **Templates**, you must create a subfolder of the **Templates** folder. When you do this, an extra tab, of the same name as the subfolder, appears in the **Templates** dialog box. Click the tab to see the templates saved within the new subfolder.*

*The predefined templates in Word (for letters, faxes, brochures and so on) are not stored in the same **Templates** folder but in subfolders of the **Templates** folder which is located in C:\Program Files\Microsoft Office\Templates.*

Creating a template from an existing document

※ If necessary, open the document concerned.

※ Set out the styles, text and layout you require.

※ Clear anything that you do not want to save with the template.

※ **File - Save As**

※ Open the **Save as type** drop-down list and click **Document Templates (*.dot)**.

*Word offers to save in the **Templates** folder.*

▨ If necessary, open the folder in which you wish to save the template.

▨ Modify the **File name** if you wish.

▨ Click the **Save** button.

📄 *To modify a template, open it with the **File - Open** command, making sure the **Document Templates (*.dot)** option is selected in the **Files of type** list. Make your required changes then save it.*

5 ▪ Linking a template to an existing document

This allows you to use the styles from another template than the one used to create the current document.

▨ Open the document that you wish to link to another template.

▨ **Tools - Templates and Add-Ins**

▨ Click the **Attach** button in the **Document template** frame.

A list of all the template files opens.

▨ If necessary, double-click the name of the folder containing the template.

▨ Double-click the name of the template you wish to use.

▨ Activate the **Automatically update document styles** option if you want to update the styles in the document and use the same as those in the attached template.

▨ Click **OK**.

*The **Style** list on the toolbar now contains the styles attached to the template.*

▨ Apply the template's styles as you wish.

DOCUMENT CONTENTS AND PRESENTATION
Exercise 1.2: Styles and templates

Below, you can see **Practice Exercise** 1.2. This exercise is made up of 5 steps. If you do not know how to do one of the steps, go back to the title that corresponds to that particular lesson. When you have finished, you can check your work by reading the **Solution** that follows.

Steps in the exercise that are likely to be tested on the exam are preceded by this symbol: ▦. However, it is a good idea to complete all the steps in the exercise, to ensure that you have understood all the points discussed in the lesson.

☞ **Practice Exercise 1.2**

*To work on practice exercise 1.2, open the **1-2 Florida Tour 1.doc** document, located in the **MOUS Word 2002 Expert** folder.*

▦ 1. Create a style called **Tour** based on the presentation of the paragraph **TOUR 1: FLORIDA DISCOVERY**.

▦ 2. Apply the style called **Intro** to the paragraph starting **This itinerary...**; to the text **Atlantic Coast** that appears in this same paragraph, apply the character style called **Blue characters**.

▦ 3. Modify the **Intro** style, including a justified alignment in it. Save your document.

4. From the open document, save a template containing only the current list of styles. Save this template in the **MOUS Templates** folder, which is in your **Templates** folder, and call it **1-2 Florida Tour.dot**. Close the document template.

5. Open the **1-2 Florida Tour 2.doc** in the **MOUS Word 2002 Expert** folder and link it to the template you just created (**1-2 Florida Tour.dot**). While making the link, make sure you choose to update the style automatically. Next, apply styles to the first paragraphs, as described below:

On this paragraph:	Apply this style:
TOUR 2: FAST FLORIDA	Tour
You have only one week...	Intro
1st day: London/Miami	Day
Fly to Miami...	Paragraph

Finish by saving and closing the document.

If you would like to practise these features more, on another document, you should work through Summary Exercise 1, on DOCUMENT CONTENTS AND PRESENTATION. You will find the summary exercises at the end of the book.

DOCUMENT CONTENTS AND PRESENTATION
Exercise 1.2: Styles and templates

It is often possible to perform a task in several different ways, but here, only the easiest solution is presented. You can go back to the corresponding lesson if you want to see other techniques you could use.

Solution to Exercise 1.2

1. To create a style based on the presentation of the paragraph "TOUR 1: FLORIDA DISCOVERY", start by clicking this paragraph.
   Click the name of the active style (**Normal + Verdana...**) in the **Style** list box on the **Formatting** toolbar and enter **Tour** as the style name. Confirm your new style by pressing the ⏎ key.

2. To apply the style called Intro to the paragraph starting "This itinerary...", click that paragraph, open the **Style** list box on the **Formatting** toolbar and click the style called **Intro**.

   To apply the character style called Blue characters to the text "Atlantic Coast", select the text **Atlantic Coast**, open the **Style** list box on the **Formatting** toolbar and click the style called **Blue characters**.

3. To modify the Intro style, click the paragraph starting "This itinerary...", to which this style has been applied, and apply a justified alignment to it by clicking the 🔳 tool button on the **Formatting** toolbar.
   If it is not visible, show the **Styles and Formatting** task pane by clicking the 🔠 tool button. Point to the style called **Intro**, click the 🔽 button then choose the **Update to Match Selection** option.
   Click the 💾 tool button to save your document.

4. To create a document template from another document, saving only the styles, select the entire contents of the document with the **Edit - Select All** command and delete them by pressing the Del key.

Use the **File - Save As** command and in the **Save as type** list box, choose the **Document Template (*.dot)** option.

Double-click the **MOUS Templates** folder.

In the **File name** text box, enter the text **1-2 Florida Tour.dot** then click the **Save** button.

To close the template, use the **File - Close** command.

5. To open the 1-2 Florida Tour 2.doc document and link it to your newly-created template, click the ⬚ tool button. In the **Files of type** list, choose the **Word Documents (*.doc)** option then select the **MOUS Word 2002 Expert** folder using the **Look in** list. Double-click the **1-2 Florida Tour 2.doc** document.

Use the **Tools - Templates and Add-Ins** command and in the **Document template** frame, click the **Attach** button. Double-click the **MOUS Templates** folder then the **1-2 Florida Tour.dot** template.

Tick the **Automatically update document styles** option then click the **OK** button.

Apply styles from the attached template to the first paragraphs in the document, as described below: to do this, click in the paragraph concerned, open the **Style** list on the **Formatting** toolbar and click the style you want to apply:

On the paragraph starting with:	Apply this style :
TOUR 2: FAST FLORIDA	Tour
You only have one week…	Intro
1st day: London/Miami	Day
Fly to Miami…	Paragraph

To save then close the document, click the ⬚ tool button then use the **File - Close** command.

DOCUMENT CONTENTS AND PRESENTATION
Exercise 1.2: Styles and templates

DOCUMENT CONTENTS AND PRESENTATION
Lesson 1.3: Tables

📖 1 ▪ **Sorting a list or a table**

Sorting a list

A list is composed of a series of paragraphs that contain text presented in columns (called fields), separated by tab stops or semi-colons. Here is an example:

```
L  ·1·1·1·2·1·3·1·4·1·5·1·6·1·7·1·8·1·9·1·10·1·11·1·12·1·13·
   ¶
   SURNAME → FIRST·NAME → DEPARTMENT → EXTENSION¶
   Alderman →  Melissa   →  Accounting   →  301¶
   Andrews  →  Frances   →  Sales      →  311¶
   Barnett  →  John      →  Multimedia   →  309¶
   Barton   →  James     →  Personnel    →  305¶
   Charles  →  Terry     →  Sales      →  312¶
   Dell     →  Pamela    →  Sales      →  313¶
   Dorcas   →  Michelle  →  Personnel    →  305¶
   Marshall →  Anthony   →  Accounting   →  302¶
   Nelson   →  Ashley    →  Multimedia   →  308¶
   Precht   →  William   →  Warehouse    →  315¶
   Rowe     →  David     →  Warehouse    →  315¶
   Sanders  →  Heather   →  Sales      →  310¶
   Townsend →  Yolanda   →  Office     →  303¶
```

» Select the list of paragraphs you want to sort.

» **Table - Sort**

Notice that you can sort according to three different criteria.

» If the first paragraph in the selection contains headers and is not to be sorted, activate the **Header row** option in the **My list has** frame.

» In the first list in the **Sort by** frame, choose the field number or header by which you wish to sort.

» In the **Type** list, choose the kind of data you want to sort: **Text**, **Number** or **Date** (for data made up of at least a day and month or a month and year).

» Activate the appropriate option to indicate you want to sort in **Ascending** or **Descending** order.

* If, in the column by which you are sorting, several rows contain the same data, define a second set of criteria in the first **Then by** frame, following the same principles.

* If required, define a third set of criteria in the second **Then by** frame.

* Click **OK** to start sorting.

*You can change the field separators by using the options in the **Separate fields at** frame in the **Sort Options** dialog box (**Table - Sort - Options** button).*

Sorting a table

* In the table, select the items you want to sort. If you want to sort the whole table, you do not need to select it, just click inside it.

* **Table - Sort**

* If the first paragraph in the selection contains headers and is not to be sorted, activate the **Header row** option in the **My list has** frame.

* In the first list in the **Sort by** frame, choose the column number or header by which you wish to sort.

* In the **Type** list, choose the kind of data you want to sort: **Text**, **Number** or **Date** (for data made up of at least a day and month or a month and year).

* Activate the appropriate option to indicate you want to sort in **Ascending** or **Descending** order.

* If, in the column by which you are sorting, several rows contain the same data, define a second set of criteria in the first **Then by** frame, following the same principles.

* If required, define a third set of criteria in the second **Then by** frame.

* When you have defined all your criteria, click **OK**.

If you have sorted your table and you are not satisfied with the result, you can click the [icon] tool button to restore the initial order.

*You can also use the [icon] or [icon] tool buttons on the **Tables and Borders** toolbar to sort the contents of the active column in ascending or descending order.*

Sorting a single column in a table

☀ Select the column you want to sort.

☀ **Table - Sort**

☀ Keep **Column** as the active choice in the first **Sort by** list.

☀ In the **Type** list, choose the kind of data you are sorting: **Text**, **Number** or **Date**.

☀ Click the **Options** button.

☀ Activate the **Sort column only** option in the option in the **Sort options** frame.

☀ Click **OK** twice.

2 ▪ Merging/splitting cells

Merging cells

This action transforms several cells into a single cell. For example:

these cells have been merged		1st Quarter			2nd Quarter		
		Jan	Feb	Mar	Apr	May	June
Category A	Juniors	15	10	5	14	9	12
	Seniors	12	9	6	11	5	13
Category B	Juniors	8	9	2	7	8	6
	Seniors	12	10	3	11	7	10

☀ Select the cells you want to merge.

☀ **Table - Merge Cells**

You can also click the tool button on the ***Tables and Borders*** *toolbar.*

☀ If necessary, display the **Tables and Borders** toolbar by clicking the tool button.

☀ Click the tool button.

The mouse pointer takes the form of an eraser.

» Drag to "erase" the line separating the cells you want to merge.

» Click the [tool button] tool button again to deactivate this tool.

Splitting cells

This technique, the opposite of merging, allows you to divide one cell into several cells.

» Select the cells you want to split.

» **Table - Split Cells**

*You can also click the [tool button] tool button on the **Tables and Borders** toolbar.*

» In the corresponding text boxes, specify the **Number of columns** and/or **Number of rows** that you want to create.

» Tick the **Merge cells before split** option if you want to merge all the selected cells into one before splitting the resulting cell into rows and columns. If this option is not active, each cell in the selection will be divided into the stated number of columns or rows.

» Click **OK**.

» Click the [tool button] tool button on the **Tables and Borders** toolbar.

The mouse pointer takes the form of a pencil.

» Drag the pointer (the pencil) horizontally or vertically to create new cell divisions.

» When you have finished splitting the cells, click the [tool button] tool button again to deactivate this tool.

3 ▪ Adding up a column/row

▪ If necessary, display the **Tables and Borders** toolbar by clicking the ⊞ tool button.

▪ Click the cell in which you want to display the result.

▪ Click the Σ tool button.

➤ Recommended route for tour of main tourist attractions:

Start	Arrive	Distance in kilometres
Miami	Key West	250
Key West	Naples	350
Naples	Sarasota	170
Sarasota	Orlando	230
Orlando	Cape Canaveral	100
Cape Canaveral	Miami	350
Distance travelled	in kilometres	1450
	in miles (1 mile = 1.609 km)	

By default, Word first adds the cells above the result cell.

4 ▪ Managing a table as in a spreadsheet

Basic principles

▪ Each column is identified by a letter (the first column is A, the second column is B and so on) and each row is identified by a number (the first row is 1, the second is 2 and so on).
The reference of a cell is defined by associating the column letter and the row number (A2, B5, etc.).

▪ To refer to adjacent cells, give the reference of the first cell, type a colon (:) and the reference of the last cell (e.g. C2:C4).
To refer to non-adjacent cells, use a semi-colon (;) as a separator (e.g. B5;D5).

Entering a calculation formula

▪ Click the cell in which the result should appear.

▪ **Table - Formula**

▪ If necessary, delete everything currently in the **Formula** box, except the = sign.

▪ In the **Formula** box, enter your formula after the = sign, using the cell references and the following mathematical operators:

-	to subtract,
/	to divide,
*	to multiply,
%	to calculate a percentage,
^	to calculate to the power of,
+	to add.

▪ If necessary, choose a **Number format** in the corresponding list.

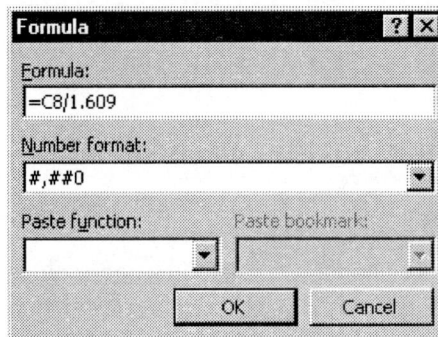

▪ Click **OK**.

Using a calculation function in a table

※ Click the cell in which the result should appear.

※ **Table - Formula**

※ If necessary, delete everything currently in the **Formula** box, except the = sign.

※ In the **Paste function** list, choose the function that corresponds to the calculation you want to make.

※ In the **Formula** box, indicate the items to which the formula will apply, by inserting the following between brackets:

ABOVE	all the cells above.
BELOW	all the cells below.
LEFT	all the cells to the left.
RIGHT	all the cells to the right.
Cell ref.:Cell ref.	adjacent cells.
Cell ref.;Cell ref.	non-adjacent cells.

※ If necessary, choose the **Number format** to be applied to the result.

※ Click **OK**.

Formatting a calculation result

※ **Table - Formula**

※ Create your calculation formula.

⁜ Open the **Number format** list and choose a format (the effect of each format is shown below, using the number -3637,54):

#,##0	- 3,638
#,##0.00	-3,637.54
£#,##0.00;(£#,##0.00)	(£3,637.54)
$#,##0.00;($#,##0.00)	($3,637.54)
0	-3638
0%	-3638%
0.00	-3637.54
0.00%	-3637.54%

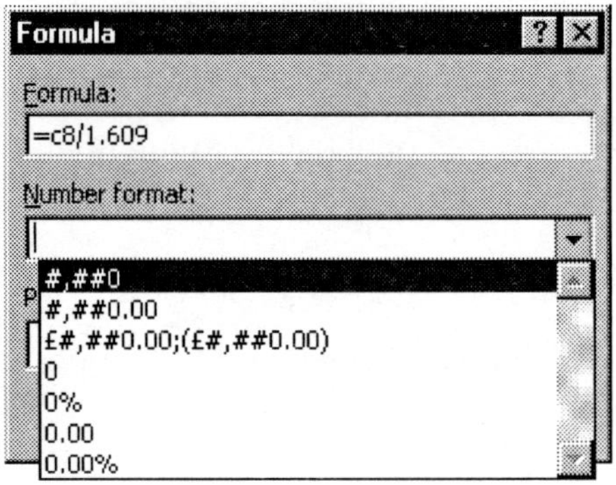

Formula ? ✕

Formula:

```
=c8/1.609
```

Number format:

```
#,##0
#,##0.00
£#,##0.00;(£#,##0.00)
0
0%
0.00
0.00%
```

⁜ Click **OK** to insert the formula in the table.

> 📄 *Calculation results are in fact **FIELD** results.*
> *Values are shown if you are in results view and not field codes view.*

5 ▪ Showing/hiding field codes

⁜ To show/hide a particular field code, place the insertion point on the field and press `Shift` `F9`.

⁜ To show/hide the field codes throughout the whole document, press `Alt` `F9`.

Start	Arrive	Distance in kilometres
Miami	Key West	250
Key West	Naples	350
Naples	Sarasota	170
Sarasota	Orlando	230
Orlando	Cape Canaveral	100
Cape Canaveral	Miami	350
Distance travelled	in kilometres	{ =SUM(ABO VE) }
	in miles (1 mile = 1.609 km)	{ =c8/1.609 \# "#,##0" }

The formulas appear between braces. Word saves the formulas and not the values, which means that if a value is changed, the result can be updated.

6 ▪ Updating a field

▪ Place the insertion point in the field you want to update.

▪ Press the F9 key.

You can also right-click the field you want to update and choose the **Update Field** *option.*

7 ▪ Embedding a Microsoft Excel worksheet into a Microsoft Word document

This technique allows you to create an object in Word that contains a Microsoft Excel worksheet (existing or new).

Embedding a new sheet

This method involves opening Excel (without leaving Word) in order to create a table.

▪ Place the insertion point where you want to insert the object.

▪ **Insert - Object - Create New** tab

▪ In the **Object type**, choose **Microsoft Excel Worksheet**.

▪ If you want the sheet to be shown as an icon and not as an Excel sheet, activate **Display as icon**.

If you activate this option, Microsoft Excel is opened in a new window; you can save the Excel worksheet you have created.

▪ Click **OK**.

*If you do not activate the **Display as icon** option in the **Object** dialog box, the worksheet appears in a frame with a hatched border. The Microsoft Excel menus and toolbars replace those from Word. Otherwise, the Excel application starts and the worksheet appears in its own window.*

▪ Enter your work in the object, using the Excel options and features; Excel acts as a server application.

When you have finished, click the Word document to see the object within Word.

You can also use the [icon] *tool button to embed a new worksheet. Click this tool button and, holding down the mouse, drag over the number of columns and rows you want in the table then release the mouse button.*

Embedding an existing worksheet

This feature allows you to embed a complete worksheet from an existing Excel workbook.

Place the insertion point where you want to insert the object.

DOCUMENT CONTENTS AND PRESENTATION
Lesson 1.3: Tables

* **Insert - Object**

* Click the **Create from File** tab.

* In the **File name** box, enter the name of the Microsoft Excel workbook that contains the worksheet you want to embed or use the **Browse** button to select the workbook.

* Tick the **Link to file** check box if you want to link the embedded object with its source file.

* If you wish, activate the **Display as icon** option so the sheet will appear in the document as an icon and not as an Excel sheet.

* Click **OK**.

The worksheet appears in the Microsoft Word document. This object can be managed like any other Word object.

If you activate the **Display as icon** option in the **Object** dialog box, the sheet appears like this:

C:\MOUS Word 2002 Expert\1-3 Average t

If the workbook contains several sheets, Excel will only embed the sheet that is active when the workbook is opened.

⌨8 ▪ Copying Microsoft Excel data into Microsoft Word including a link

* Open the Microsoft Excel application and the workbook that contains the data you want to copy.

* Select the Microsoft Excel data that you want to copy (table, chart etc.).

* **Edit - Copy** or ▣ or ⌨ C

* Open the Microsoft Word application and the document into which you want to copy the data.

* Place the insertion point where the data are to appear.

* **Edit - Paste Special**

* Activate the **Paste link** option.

* Select the format in which the data are to be pasted from the **As** list.

* Click **OK**.

The data appear at the insertion point. Any changes made to the Microsoft Excel data will be carried over immediately to Microsoft Word as updating is automatic by default.

▣9 ▪ Editing a Microsoft Excel worksheet inserted in a Microsoft Word document

The way in which you make changes to a worksheet depends on how it was inserted in the Word document.

Editing a linked worksheet

▪ **Edit - Links**

▪ Click the linked object, then the **Open Source** button.

You can also double-click the Microsoft Excel worksheet object.

The Microsoft Excel application starts and opens the workbook containing the worksheet.

▫ Make your changes.

The changes you make are applied to the object in the Word document straight away.

▫ Close the Microsoft Excel application with **File - Quit** or click the source document.

If you close Excel without saving the workbook, the changes you made are still saved in the Word document. In this case, you need to make a manual update by clicking the Excel worksheet object and pressing F9 *.*

📄 *Links are, by default, updated automatically if the **Update automatic links at Open** option is active under the **General** tab of the **Options** dialog box (**Tools - Options**). To change the type of update, click the object concerned if necessary then use **Edit - Links** and choose the **Update** type: **Automatic** or **Manual**. You can update a manual link by pressing* F9 *.*

Editing an embedded worksheet

▫ Double-click the embedded object, which represents the worksheet you want to modify, to open it.

If the object has been embedded as a worksheet, Microsoft Excel menus and toolbars replace those of Word and the worksheet appears in a hatched border. If you embedded the object as an icon, Excel opens and the worksheet is shown in the Excel window.

▫ Make the required changes to the embedded object.

▫ If you have been editing an embedded object in Word, click anywhere in the document (outside the object) to resume working in Word.
If you have been editing the embedded object in a separate Excel window, return to Word by using **File - Exit** to close Excel.

When you embed a worksheet selected from an existing workbook, the entire workbook is inserted into the document but you can see only one sheet. To see other sheets, double-click the Microsoft Excel object, then click the worksheet you want to see.

*If you want to edit a Microsoft Excel object but do not have that application installed on your computer, select the object and use **Edit - Worksheet Object - Convert** and choose a file format that is managed by an application you do have.*

*You can also click the object and use **Edit - Worksheet Object** and choose **Open** to make changes directly in Microsoft Excel or choose **Edit** if you want to remain in Word to make your changes.*

DOCUMENT CONTENTS AND PRESENTATION
Exercise 1.3: Table

Below, you can see **Practice Exercise** 1.3. This exercise is made up of 9 steps. If you do not know how to do one of the steps, go back to the title that corresponds to that particular lesson. When you have finished, you can check your work by reading the **Solution** that follows.

Steps in the exercise that are likely to be tested on the exam are preceded by this symbol: ⊞. However, it is a good idea to complete all the steps in the exercise, to ensure that you have understood all the points discussed in the lesson.

☞ Practice Exercise 1.3

To work on practice exercise 1.3, open the **1-3 Florida in Numbers.doc** document, located in the **MOUS Word 2002 Expert** folder.

⊞ 1. Sort the first table in the document in ascending order by number of inhabitants.

2. Merge the two cells with an orange background, that you can see in the second table in the document.

⊞ 3. In the document's second table, add the distances in kilometres and display the result in the cell with the green background.

⊞ 4. In the second table, convert the total number of kilometres into miles and display the result in the pink-coloured cell (1 mile equals 1.609 kilometres). Apply a thousands format to the result of this formula.

5. Show all the existing field codes in the document.

6. Hide all the field codes in the document then, in the second table, correct the number of kilometres between **Miami** and **Key West** to 260 kilometres. Next, update the two calculation formulas in this table.

7. Embed a new Excel worksheet in page 2 of the document, underneath the **Average temperatures in Miami (in °C)** paragraph. Enter the data shown below:

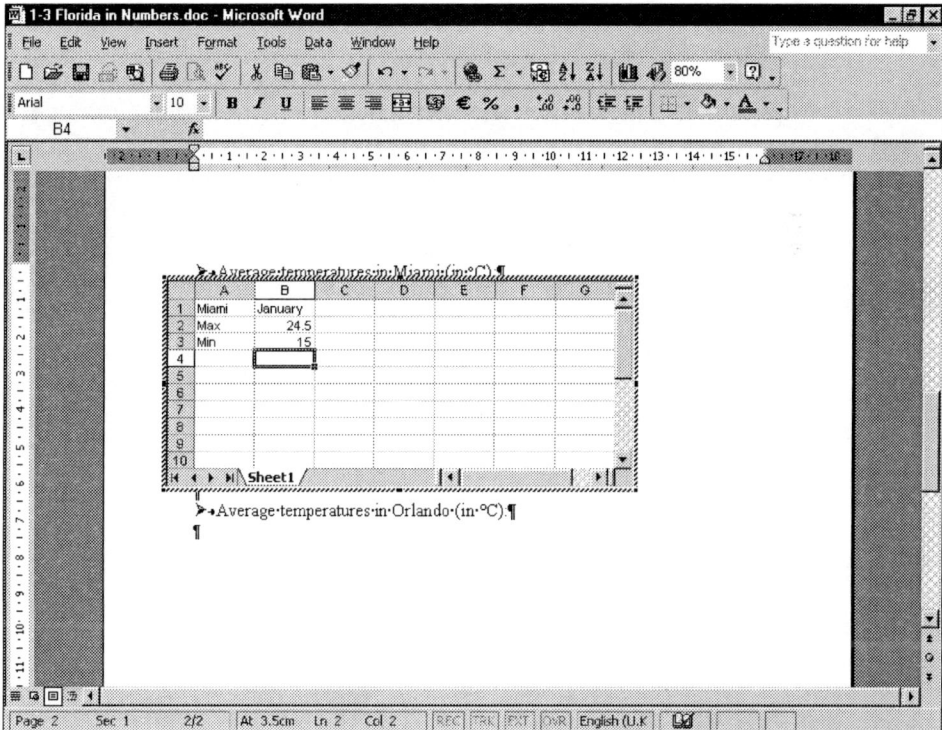

Now, undo this insertion and in its place, embed the active sheet from the **1-3 Average temperatures** workbook, which can be found in the **MOUS Word 2002 Expert** folder. Insert the object without linking.

8. Copy, with a link, cells A1 to M4 from the worksheet called **Orlando** in the **1-3 Average temperatures** workbook (in the **MOUS Word 2002 Expert** folder) and paste this data below the **Average temperatures in Orlando (in °C)** paragraph at the end of the document. Close Microsoft Excel, saving the changes made to the workbook and return to the **1-3 Florida in Numbers** document.

DOCUMENT CONTENTS AND PRESENTATION
Exercise 1.3: Table

▦ 9. The maximum January temperature in Orlando is actually 22°C. Change this information then leave Excel, saving the changes to the workbook. If necessary, activate the **1-3 Florida in Numbers** Word document again and close it, saving the changes you have made.

If you would like to practise these features more, on another document, you should work through Summary Exercise 1, on DOCUMENT CONTENTS AND PRESENTATION. You will find the summary exercises at the end of the book.

It is often possible to perform a task in several different ways, but here, only the easiest solution is presented. You can go back to the corresponding lesson if you want to see other techniques you could use.

Solution to Exercise 1.3

1. To sort the first table in ascending order by number of inhabitants, click in the table and use the **Table - Sort** command.
   In the first list box in the **Sort by** frame, select the **Number of inhabitants** column header.
   Select the **Number** option in the **Type** list, then make sure the **Ascending** option is active.
   In the **My list has** frame, activate the **Header row** option.
   Click **OK**.

2. To merge the two cells with an orange background, which are in the document's second table, select these two cells then use the **Table - Merge Cells** command.

3. To add the distances in kilometres and show the result in the green-coloured cell in the second table, start by clicking that cell.

   If necessary, show the **Tables and Borders** toolbar by clicking the [tool icon] tool button.
   Click the [Σ] tool button.

4. To convert the total number of kilometres into miles, in the pink cell in the second table, click this cell then use the **Table - Formula** command.
   Delete any information that may appear in the **Formula** text box except the = sign.
   Place the insertion point after the = sign in the **Formula** text box and type **C8/1.609**.

Open the **Number format** list and select the **#,##0** format.
Click **OK**.

5. To show all the field codes in the document, press the [Alt][F9] keys.

6. To hide all the field codes in the document, press the [Alt][F9] keyboard shortcut again.

To replace the number of kilometres between **Miami** and **Key West**, select **250** and type **260**.

To update the two calculation formulas in the table, click the first formula (whose result is 1450) and press [F9]. Next, click the second formula (whose result is 901) and press [F9] again.

7. To embed a new worksheet in page 2 of the document, underneath the "Average temperatures in Miami (in °C)" paragraph, click the empty paragraph that follows.
Use the **Insert - Object** command then click the **Create New** tab.
In the **Object type** list, select the **Microsoft Excel Worksheet** option and click **OK**.

Enter the following data:

Once you have finished, click the Microsoft Word document and use **Edit - Undo Object**.

To embed the active worksheet in the "1-3 Average temperatures" workbook in the same place, use the **Insert - Object** command.

Click the **Create from File** tab and then the **Browse** button.

Select the **1-3 Average temperatures.xls** workbook in the **MOUS Word 2002 Expert** folder then click the **Insert** button. Click **OK** to insert the worksheet.

8. To copy cells A1 to M4 from the "Orlando" worksheet in the "1-3 Average temperatures" workbook at the end of the document, creating a link with the source worksheet, start the Microsoft Excel application.

DOCUMENT CONTENTS AND PRESENTATION
Exercise 1.3: Table

Open the workbook called **1-3 Average temperatures.xls** which is in the **MOUS Word 2002 Expert** folder.

Click the **Orlando** tab then select cells **A1** to **M4**.

Click the ▣ tool button.

On the Windows taskbar, click the button that corresponds to the Microsoft Word document called **1-3 Florida in Numbers.doc** then press Ctrl End to place the insertion point at the end of the document.

Use the **Edit - Paste Special** command and tick the **Paste link** check box.

In the **As** list, choose **Microsoft Excel Worksheet Object** then click **OK**.

To close the Microsoft Excel application, click the button on the taskbar corresponding to the **1-3 Average temperatures.xls** workbook and use the **File - Exit** command then click **Yes** on the message that asks if you want to save your changes. If necessary, return to the **1-3 Florida in Numbers.doc** Word document by clicking its button on the taskbar.

▣ 9. To change the maximum temperature for Orlando in the month of January, which should be 22°C, double-click the last table in the document (showing the temperatures for Orlando): the Microsoft Excel application opens in a new window.

Click cell **B2** in the **Orlando** worksheet, enter **22** then press the ↵ key.

To close the Microsoft Excel application, saving the changes made to the workbook, use the **File - Exit** command then click **Yes** on the message asking you if you want to save your changes.

If necessary, return to the **1-3 Florida in Numbers.doc** document by clicking the corresponding button on the taskbar.

To close and save the 1-3 Florida in Numbers.doc document, use **File - Close** and click **Yes** on the message asking you if you want to save your changes.

DOCUMENT CONTENTS AND PRESENTATION
Lesson 1.4: Charts

DOCUMENT CONTENTS AND PRESENTATION
Lesson 1.4: Charts

1 ▪ Creating a chart based on Microsoft Excel or Microsoft Access data

Starting Microsoft Graph

▪ Place the insertion point where the chart should appear.

▪ Insert - Object

▪ Double-click the **Microsoft Graph Chart** option in the **Object type** list.

*After a few seconds, a window called **Datasheet** appears, containing the data represented in the chart. A chart also appears, surrounded by a hatched border. The data currently shown in the datasheet and chart are sample data.*

The menus and toolbars belong to the Microsoft Graph 2002 application.

▪ It is a good idea to reorganise the objects on your screen, by moving the **Datasheet** window so that you can see the chart properly.

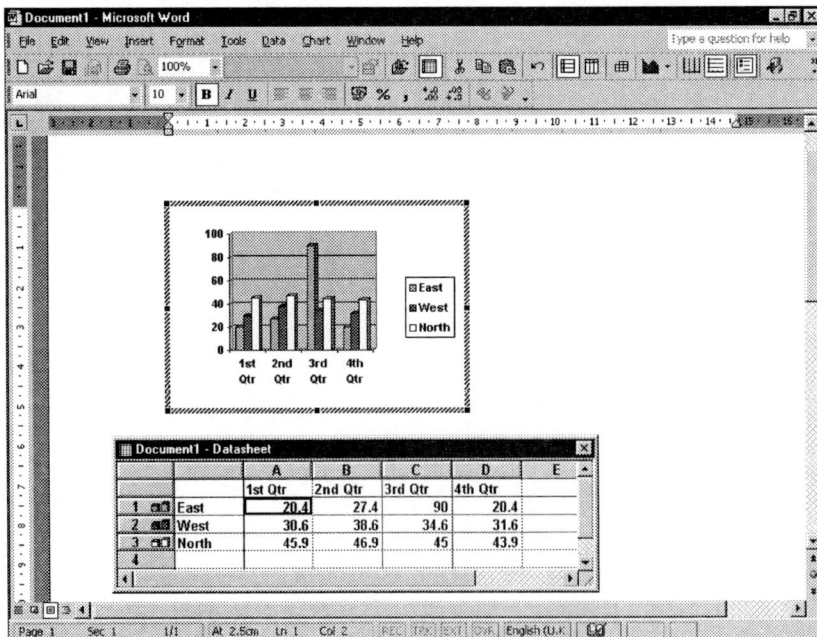

▪ Insert the data you want to represent into the datasheet then define the chart settings (cf. below).

Clearing the datasheet cells

▪ Select the cells you want to clear.

▪ **Edit - Clear**

▪ Choose whether you want to clear **All**, the **Contents** or the **Formats** of the cells.

The chart no longer shows the numerical data but Microsoft Graph still considers there to be four categories (shown on the x-axis) and three series (shown as columns).

Deleting rows/columns in the datasheet

By default, four categories and three data series are active in a chart datasheet. If your chart uses less than this, you must delete the extra rows (data series) or columns (categories) in the datasheet before entering your data.

▪ Select the rows/columns you want to delete by dragging over the corresponding row or column headers.

▪ **Edit - Delete** or Ctrl - (alphanumeric keyboard) or Del

Importing a Microsoft Excel worksheet into a chart

▪ If you have left Microsoft Graph, double-click the chart object to open it.

▪ Click the first cell in the datasheet.

▪ **Edit - Import File**

▪ In the **Look in** list, choose the drive and the folder that contain the workbook you want to import.

*The **File of type** box shows **Microsoft Excel Files (*.xl* ; *.xls ; *.xlc ; *.xlt)**.*

▪ Double-click the name of the Excel workbook you want to import.

⬥ If you have selected an Excel workbook created with version 5.0 or later, select the sheet you want to import.

You can import only one worksheet.

You can import up to 4000 rows and 4000 columns of imported data but you can only have 255 data series in a chart.

⬥ To import all the data in the worksheet, click the **Entire sheet** option in the **Import** frame.
To import only part of the data, click the **Range** option and enter the cell references as follows: **First cell:Last cell**.

⬥ Make sure the **Overwrite existing cells** check box is ticked if you want to replace all the data in the datasheet with the imported data.

⬥ Click **OK**.

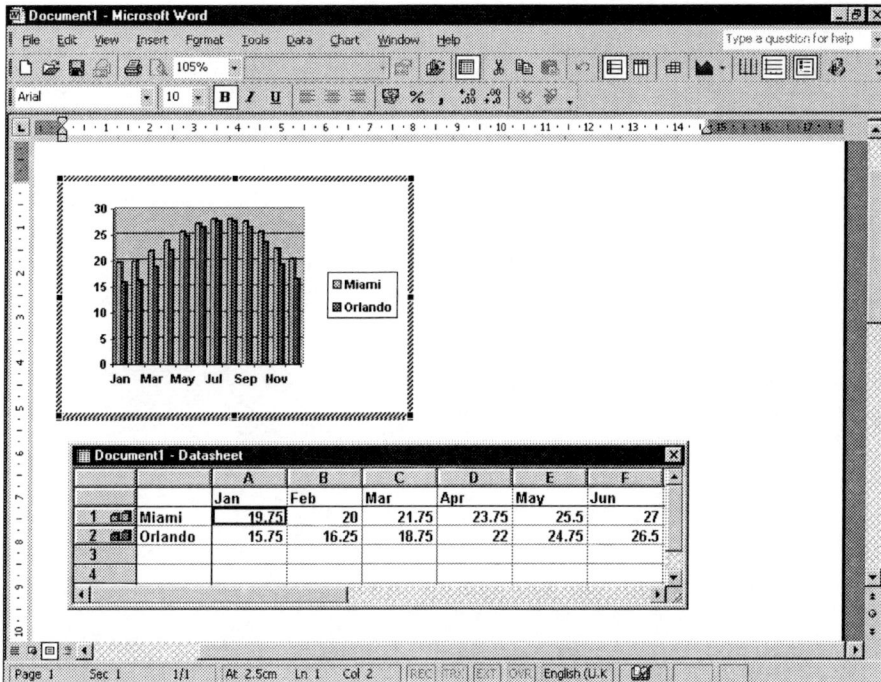

The datasheet and the chart are immediately updated.

Copying Microsoft Access data into a chart

You can copy data from an Access query or pivot table form into your Word chart.

* Open the Microsoft Access application then the database containing the data you want to copy.

* Click **Queries** or **Forms** in the objects bar, depending on whether you are copying from a query or pivot table form.

* Double-click the name of the query or pivot table form to open it.

You will obtain a more correct representation of data in the chart by copying data from a crosstab query, in which the row headers will represent the chart's data series, the column headers will represent the chart's categories (on the x-axis) and the values will represent the chart's numerical data.

⁕ If you have opened a query, select the data you wish to copy into the chart.
If you have opened a pivot table form, hold down the Ctrl A keys to select it; if the pivot table form includes a filter field, this will also be selected. You can make any changes you require at a later time in the chart datasheet (such as deleting or moving rows and columns).

⁕ **Edit - Copy** or 📋 or Ctrl C

⁕ Click the taskbar button that corresponds to the Word document into which you are copying the data; this will open the document.

⁕ If necessary, activate the Microsoft Graph application by double-clicking the chart object.

⁕ Click the first cell in the datasheet.

⁕ **Edit - Paste** or 📋 or Ctrl V

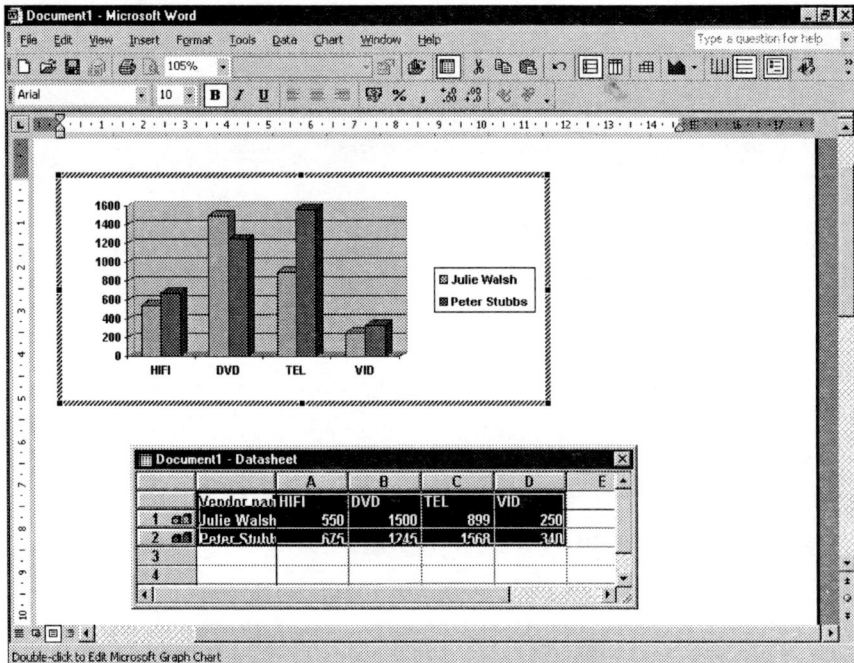

The datasheet and the chart are immediately updated.

* Make any necessary changes to the datasheet (delete or move rows or columns).

Leaving the Microsoft Graph application

* Click outside the datasheet or chart, anywhere in the Word document.

📄 *You can treat a chart as any other drawing object; it can be moved, resized and so on.*

▣2 • Editing a chart

Opening Microsoft Graph

* Double-click the chart you want to modify or select it and use the **Edit - Chart Object - Edit** command.
* Make your changes to the chart or datasheet.

Indicating whether the series are in rows or columns

* If necessary, open the Microsoft Graph application by double-clicking the chart object.
* **Data - Series in Rows** or **Series in Columns**

Changing the chart type

* If necessary, open the Microsoft Graph application by double-clicking the chart object.
* **Chart - Chart Type**

  The names of all the main chart types are listed.

* Select the required **Chart type** from the list.

DOCUMENT CONTENTS AND PRESENTATION
Lesson 1.4: Charts

* In the **Chart sub-type** box, double-click the type you want to use.

Managing the chart legend

* If necessary, open the Microsoft Graph application by double-clicking the chart object.

* **Chart - Chart Options**

* Click the **Legend** tab.

* Choose to display or hide the legend by ticking (or deactivating) the **Show legend** option.

* Choose where you want to position the legend by activating the appropriate option in the **Placement** frame.

* Click **OK**.

Adding a title to the chart/an axis

* If necessary, open the Microsoft Graph application by double-clicking the chart object.

* **Chart - Chart Options**

* Click the **Titles** tab.

* Enter the title you want to add in the appropriate text box.

* Click **OK**.

Changing the formatting of a chart item

* If necessary, open the Microsoft Graph application by double-clicking the chart object.

* Click to select the item; to select an axis, click one of its labels.

  Any selected item is surrounded by selection handles. Black handles indicate that the item can be moved and/or resized.

⁂ Open the **Format** menu and activate the first option in this menu, which corresponds to the name of the selected item, or double-click the item you want to modify.

⁂ Activate the tab that corresponds to the feature you want to change.

*The **Format** dialog box displays different tabs according to the selected item.*

⁂ Make the required formatting changes.

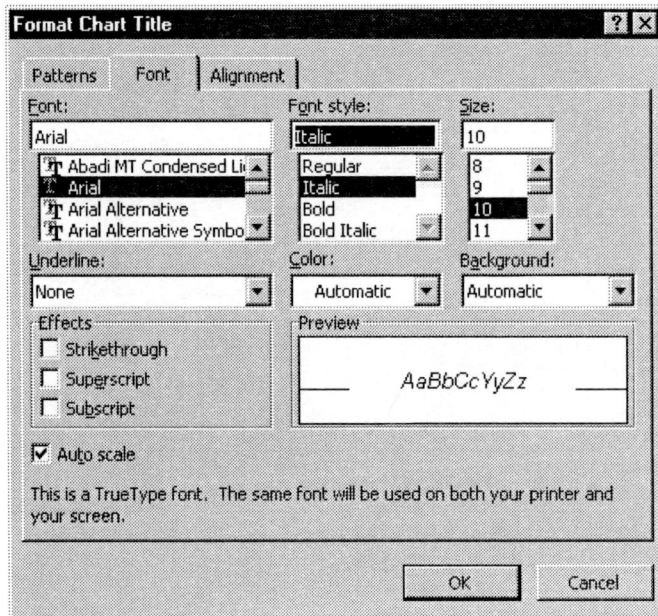

⁂ Click **OK**.

Below, you can see **Practice Exercise** 1.4. This exercise is made up of 2 steps. If you do not know how to do one of the steps, go back to the title that corresponds to that particular lesson. When you have finished, you can check your work by reading the **Solution** that follows.

All the steps in this exercise are likely to be tested during the exam.

Practice Exercise 1.4

1. Create a new document, go into Microsoft Graph and clear all the cells on the chart datasheet. Next, import the data in cells **A1** to **M3** from the **Average temperatures** worksheet in the **1-4 Florida Temperatures.xls** workbook, which is in the **MOUS Word 2002 Expert** folder. You should obtain the following result:

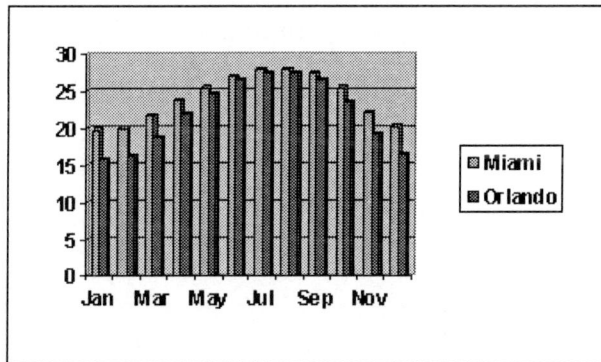

Quit the Microsoft Graph application then resize the chart object until it is **16 cm** (6 ½ inches) wide and **8 cm** (3 ¼ inches) high.

▦ 2. Change the chart, using the following example to guide you:

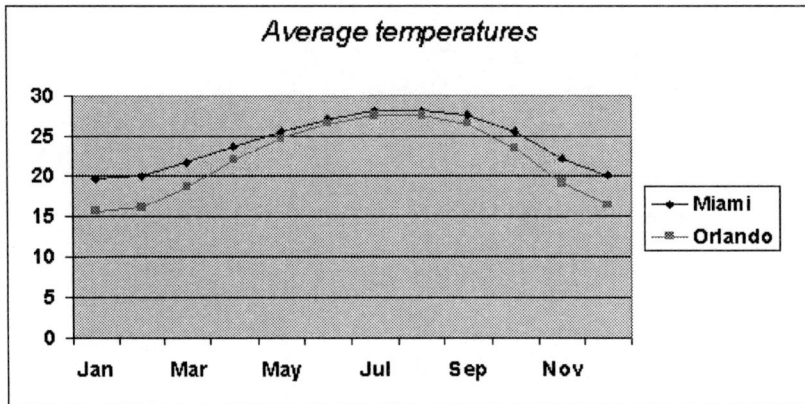

Average temperatures

You have to:

- change the chart type: this is a **Line** chart,

- add the title **Average temperatures** to the chart,

- apply an italics format to this title.

Leave the Microsoft Graph application. Save your document in the **MOUS Word 2002 Expert** folder, under the name of **1-4 Florida Temperatures Chart.doc** then close the document.

If you would like to practise these features more, on another document, you should work through Summary Exercise 1, on DOCUMENT CONTENTS AND PRESENTATION. You will find the summary exercises at the end of the book.

It is often possible to perform a task in several different ways, but here, only the easiest solution is presented. You can go back to the corresponding lesson if you want to see other techniques you could use.

Solution to Exercise 1.4

1. To create a new document, click the ☐ tool button.
   To open Microsoft Graph, use the **Insert - Object** command then double-click the **Microsoft Graph Chart** in the **Object type** list.

   To clear the entire contents of the datasheet, drag from the first cell in the sheet to cell **D3** then use the **Edit - Clear - All** command.

   To import data from cells A1 to M3 in the "Average temperatures" sheet in the 1-4 Florida Temperatures.xls workbook (located in the MOUS Word 2002 Expert folder), click the first cell in the datasheet. Use the **Edit - Import File** command, double-click the **MOUS Word 2002 Expert** folder then double-click the **1-4 Florida Temperatures.xls** workbook. Under **Select sheet from workbook**, select the **Average temperatures** worksheet and click **OK**.

   To leave the Microsoft Graph application, click anywhere in the Word document, outside the chart or datasheet.

   To increase the size of the chart object so it measures approximately 16 cm (6 ½ in) wide by 8 cm (3 ¼ in) high, click the chart to select it. Point to the black square (the selection handle) on the right edge and drag towards the right until the chart is 16 cm (6 ½ in) wide. Point to the selection handle on the bottom edge and drag down until the chart is 8 cm (3 ¼ in) high.

2. To modify the chart, double-click it to start the Microsoft Graph application.
To change the chart type, activate the **Chart - Chart Type** command, select **Line** in the **Chart type** list then double-click the second sub-type in the first column.

To add the "Average temperatures" title to the chart, use the **Chart - Chart Options** command then if necessary, click the **Titles** tab. Click the **Chart title** text box, if necessary, enter **Average temperatures** then click **OK**.

To apply italic type to the chart title, click the title to select it, use the **Format - Selected Chart Title** command and click the **Font** tab. Choose Italic in the **Font style** list then click **OK**.

To close the Microsoft Graph application, click outside the datasheet and chart on the Word document.

To save the document in the MOUS Word 2002 Expert folder, as 1-4 Florida Temperatures Chart.doc, click the 🖫 tool button. Open the **Save in** list, select the drive where the **MOUS Word 2002 Expert** folder is stored, then double-click the **MOUS Word 2002 Expert** folder to open it. Enter **1-4 Florida Temperatures Chart** in the **File name** text box and click the **Save** button.
To close the 1-4 Florida Temperatures Chart.doc document, use the **File - Close** command.

DOCUMENT CONTENTS AND PRESENTATION
Lesson 1.5: Drawing objects

DOCUMENT CONTENTS AND PRESENTATION
Lesson 1.5: Drawing objects

1 ▪ Inserting a picture, a sound or a video clip

Finding and inserting a picture, a sound or a video clip

▫ If necessary, use the **Insert - Picture - Clip Art** command to display the **Insert Clip Art** task pane.

*The **Add Clips to Organizer** dialog box may appear on the screen:*

```
Add Clips to Organizer

  [icon]   Welcome to Microsoft Clip Organizer!

  Clip Organizer can catalog picture, sound, and motion files found on
  your hard disk(s) or in folders you specify.

  Click Now to catalog all media files.  Click Later to postpone this task.
  Click Options to specify folders.

  ☐ Don't show this message again

              [ Now ]      [ Later ]      [ Options... ]
```

▫ Click the **Now** button if you want to add the image, audio and video files from your hard disk into the Clip Organizer. If you do not want to do that just yet, click the **Later** button.

▫ Enter one or more words in the **Search text** box

▫ To define where the search should be carried out, open the **Search in** list and make a choice, following these guidelines: the plus (+) sign expands the hierarchy while the minus (-) sign collapses it. Click a check box to select (or deselect) the corresponding category: double-clicking selects (or deselects) that category and all its subcategories.

*The **Office Collections** category and its subcategories correspond to the image, sound and video elements installed with Office. The **Web Collections** category provides you with elements found on the Web (or more precisely on the Microsoft site). Word will only take this category into account if you have an open Internet connection.*

※ To limit the type of items being searched for (**Clip Art**, **Photographs**, **Movies** or **Sounds**), open the **Results should be** list and deselect any elements that should be excluded from the search. You can also limit the search to certain file types. To do this, click the plus (+) sign on the type of element concerned and deselect any file types that should not be included in the search.

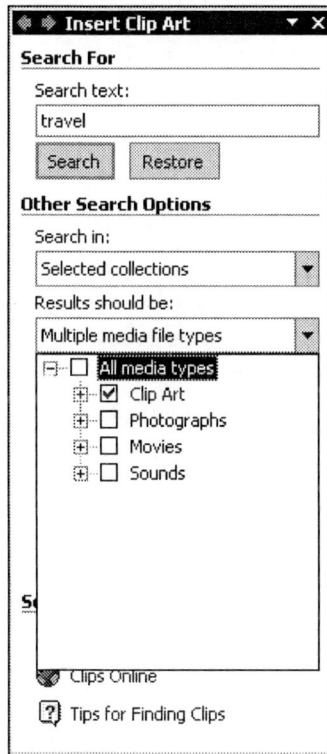

※ Click outside the list box to close it then click the **Search** button to start your search.

If you want to interrupt the search, click the **Stop** *button that appears near the bottom of the pane.*

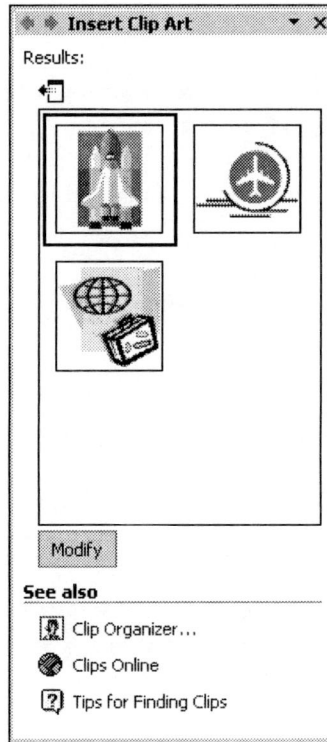

If you have included a Web search in your search, by activating **Web Collections** *in the* **Search in** *list, and if your Internet connection is open, the* [icon] *icon may appear at the bottom left of an item; this indicates that it was found on the Web.*

* When the search is finished or if you click the **Stop** button, the **Modify** button appears, which you can use to set up a new search.

* To insert one of the items found into your active document, place the insertion point where you wish to put the item then click the clip in the **Insert Clip Art** task pane.

The item appears where the insertion point was and is considered as a character, as the default wrapping style is **In line with text**. *Any changes to the text change the position of the object and the object cannot be moved freely. If you want the item to be considered as a drawing object, and not as a character, you should change its wrapping style (cf. Changing an object's wrapping).*

▪ If necessary, close the task pane by clicking the ☒ button.

▤ *When you point to an item in the* **Insert Clip Art** *task pane, a bar with an arrow appears on the right side of the clip. If you click the arrow, an options menu appears, which you can use to perform certain actions, such as* **Copy** *the item,* **Delete from Clip Organizer**, **Open Clip In** *another application, activate* **Tools on the Web**, **Copy to Collection** *(to copy to the collection of your choice),* **Edit Keywords** *that may be associated with that clip,* **Find Similar Style** *(to base the search on that style of clip) or obtain a* **Preview** *or the* **Properties** *of that clip.*

You can use the **Clips Online** *link in the task pane to search for clips directly on the Microsoft Web site.*

Using the Clip Organizer

▪ If necessary, use the **Insert - Picture - Clip Art** command to open the **Insert Clip Art** task pane.

The **Add Clips to Organizer** *dialog box may appear on the screen.*

▪ Click the **Now** button if you want to add the image, audio and video files from your hard disk into the Clip Organizer. If you do not want to do that just yet, click the **Later** button.

▪ Click the **Clip Organizer** link at the bottom of the task pane.

▪ If the **Add Clips to Organizer** dialog box appears again, choose whether or not to add the add the image, audio and video files from your hard disk into the Clip Organizer by clicking **Now** or **Later**.

DOCUMENT CONTENTS AND PRESENTATION
Lesson 1.5: Drawing objects

▪ To browse the collections of image sound or video items available in Office, expand the **Office Collections** hierarchy (click the + sign) then click the subcategory of your choice to display its contents in the right half of the window.

▪ In the **My Collections** collection, you can create and manage your own custom subcollections:

- To create a new collection within **My Collections**, select **My Collections** then use the **File - New Collection** command and enter the new collection's **Name**. Decide where to store this new collection then click **OK**.

- To copy a picture, sound or video clip into a subcollection of **My Collections**, look for the item in the **Office Collections** or **Web Collections** (if you are connected to the Internet) then drag the item from the right pane into the required subcollection in the left pane.

- To change the name of a subcollection created in **My Collections**, select the subcollection in question, then use the **Edit - Rename Collection** command. Type in the new name and press the ⏎ key.

- To delete one of the subcollections created in **My Collections**, select the subcollection concerned and press the [Del] button. Click **Yes** to confirm the deletion.

When you point to an item in the right pane of the Clip Organizer, an arrow appears on the right of it: clicking this arrow displays the list of options that were described in the section above.

▪ Close the **Clip Organizer** by clicking the [X] button on its window and if necessary, close the task pane by clicking its [X] button.

📄 *You can add a picture, sound or video clip to your document from the **Microsoft Clip Organizer** window. To do this, drag the item from the right pane of the Clip Organizer window onto the active document. The **Microsoft Clip Organizer** window disappears but is still open in the background; you can reactivate it by clicking the corresponding button on the taskbar.*

🪟2 ▪ Inserting a picture from a file

▪ Click in the document where you want to insert the picture.

▪ **Insert - Picture - From File**

▪ Go to the drive that contains the picture using the **Look in** list.

▪ Go to the folder that contains the picture you want to insert by double-clicking the folder icon.

▪ Select the picture you want to insert.

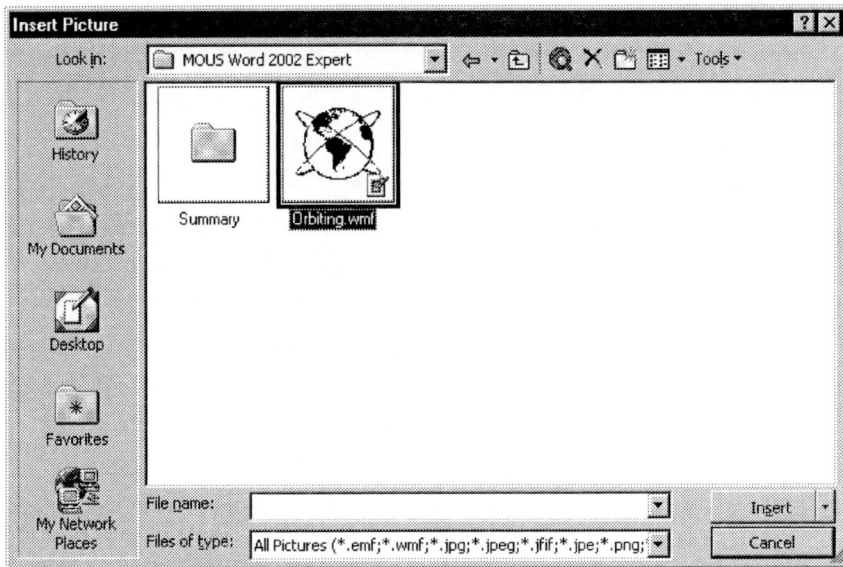

» Click the **Insert** button.

3 ▪ Creating a WordArt object

WordArt enables you to apply special typographic effects to your text, like this:

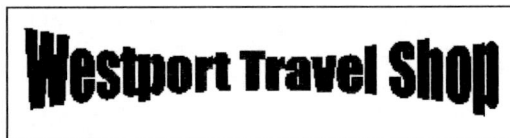

» If necessary, display the **Drawing** toolbar with the **View - Toolbars - Drawing** command or .

» If you want to create the object inside an existing drawing canvas, click that canvas to select it. Otherwise, place the insertion point where the WordArt object should appear in the document.

* Click the **A** tool button.
* Choose the effect you wish to apply.

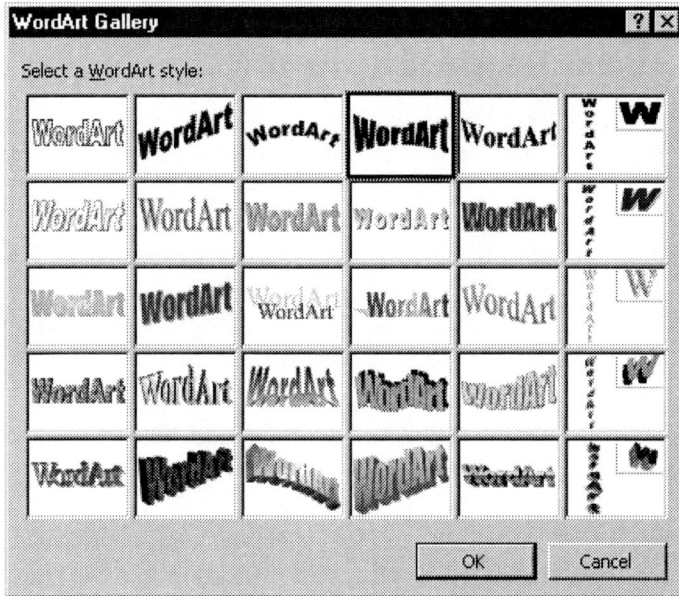

A thick black border indicates the selected effect.

* Click **OK**.
* Type in your text, using the ⏎ key to change lines.

* If you wish, format your text using the **Font** and **Size** lists and the **B** and **I** tool buttons.

* Click **OK**.

* If you have used a drawing canvas, click outside it to deactivate it.

    If the WordArt object is not entered in a drawing canvas, it appears at the insertion point and is considered as a character. Any modification to your text changes the position of the WordArt object. If you want the WordArt object to be considered as a drawing object and not as text, you should change the text wrapping for that object, which by default is **In line with text** *(cf. Changing an object's wrapping).*

4 ▪ Editing WordArt text

* If it is not selected, click the WordArt object to select it.

    The **WordArt** *toolbar appears on the screen.*

* Use the buttons on the **WordArt** toolbar to make your changes.

opens the Format dialog box ‐ ‐ text wrapping options

WordArt ▼ ✕

🄰 Edit Te_x_t... 🔲 🎨 Abc 🖼 Aa bᵇ ≡ AV ‐ character spacing options

displays the gallery ⌐
displays a choice of shape ⌐ ⌐ alignment options
makes all letters the same height ⌐ ⌐ writes the text vertically

Clicking the **Edit Text** *button displays the dialog box used for entering the WordArt text.*

🪟5 ▪ Drawing a shape

Any drawn shape is a drawing object.

Drawing a simple shape

※ If necessary, show the **Drawing** toolbar using **View - Toolbars - Drawing** or 🔳.

※ Place the insertion point where you want the drawing canvas to appear.

※ Click the tool button that corresponds to what you want to draw:

⟍	a line
⬈	an arrow
▢	a rectangle
⬭	an oval

Word inserts a drawing area called the drawing canvas at the insertion point; you can create your drawing within that area. The drawing canvas is especially useful when you are drawing several objects. The objects you create there can be organised in the document more easily and their alignment and/or spacing can be defined in relation to the drawing canvas.

※ To draw an object within the drawing canvas, position the mouse pointer within that area: if you do not wish to use the drawing canvas, place the pointer outside it.

❋ Drag to draw your shape and (if you have used one) click outside the drawing canvas to deactivate it.

If you start to draw outside the drawing canvas, it disappears automatically.

📄 To create a new object on an existing drawing canvas, select one of the objects already in that canvas then activate the required drawing tool.

As the drawing canvas is inserted at the insertion point, it is considered as a character. Any modification to your text changes the position of the drawing canvas. Furthermore, the canvas cannot be moved freely. If you want the drawing canvas to be considered as a drawing object, and not as text, you should change the text wrapping for that area, which, by default, is **In line with text** (cf. Changing an object's wrapping).

To obtain a square or circle, use the rectangle or oval tool and hold down [Shift] as you draw. To draw a rectangle/square or oval/circle from its centre (and not from one side), hold down [Ctrl] as you draw.

Creating a text box

Creating a text box allows you to position text anywhere on the page or to put paragraphs side by side.

❋ If necessary, display the **Drawing** toolbar then put the insertion point at the place where you want the text box to appear.

❋ If you want to create the text box inside an existing drawing canvas, click that canvas to select it.

❋ Click the 📄 tool button.

❋ Drag in the required place, be it inside or outside a drawing canvas, to draw the text box.

❋ Enter your text as you would enter an ordinary paragraph.

※ Click outside the box to end.

※ If you have used one, click outside the drawing canvas to deactivate it.

> Text in a text box can be formatted using the usual commands.
>
> If your text is too long to fit in the text box, you will not be able to see all of it.

Drawing an AutoShape

If necessary, display the **Drawing** toolbar then put the insertion point at the place where you want the AutoShape to appear.

※ If you want to create the AutoShape inside an existing drawing canvas, click that canvas to select it.

※ Open the **AutoShapes** drop-down list.

※ Activate the category which contains the required shape and select the shape.

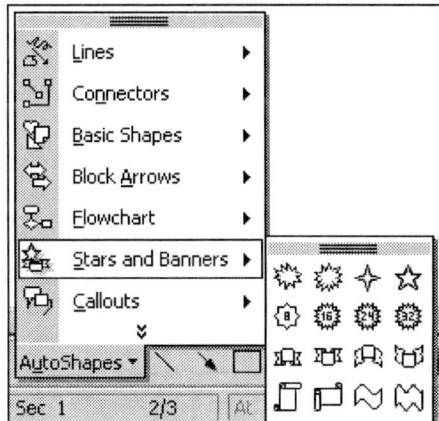

※ Drag in the required place, be it inside or outside a drawing canvas, to create the AutoShape.

※ If you have used one, click outside the drawing canvas to deactivate it.

6 ▪ Selecting objects

- Point to the object you are selecting; if you are selecting a text box, point to one of its edges.

- When the mouse pointer appears as a four-headed arrow, click.

- To select several objects, click the first object you require, hold down the [Shift] key and click the other objects you want to select.

You can also activate the 🔲 *tool and drag around the objects you are selecting. If you do this, make sure all the objects are completely enclosed within your selection rectangle.*

📄 *To cancel a selection, click outside the selected area.*

7 ▪ Deleting objects

- To delete one or more objects, select them then press the [Del] key.

- To delete all the objects on a drawing canvas, click one of the hatched borders of the drawing canvas concerned then press [Del].

8 ▪ Positioning an object

Created in a drawing canvas

This action defines the object's position in the drawing canvas.

- Select the object concerned in the drawing canvas.

- Choose the last option in the **Format** menu.

*The name of this option changes depending on the object selected (**AutoShape**, **Text Box**, **Drawing Canvas** or **Picture**).*

※ Click the **Layout** tab.

※ Give the **Horizontal** and/or **Vertical** positions of the selected object then use the **From** lists associated with each of these options to set the point from which the object should be positioned on the drawing canvas.

※ Click **OK**.

Created outside a drawing canvas

※ Select the object concerned. When you select a picture and you intend to change its position, make sure that its wrapping style is not **In line with text**.

※ Choose the last option in the **Format** menu.

※ Click the **Layout** tab.

※ Click the **Advanced** button then the **Picture Position** tab.

※ In the **Horizontal** frame, click the required type of horizontal alignment then use the corresponding lists to define exactly how the object should be positioned. You can choose from the following options:

Alignment aligns the object to the left of, centred in or to the right of the element selected in the **relative to** list box.

Book layout lines up the object in relation to the inside or outside of the page or page margins (this is useful if you need to take book binding into account).

Absolute position aligns the object horizontally: the distance given in the text box is the space left between the left side of the object and the left side of the element selected in the **to the right of** list.

※ In the **Vertical** frame, click the required type of vertical alignment then use the corresponding lists to define exactly how the object should be positioned. You can choose from these two options:

Alignment aligns the object relative to the top, centre, bottom, inside or outside edge of the element selected in the **relative to** list box.

Absolute position aligns the object with the element selected in the **below** list; the amount of space specified in the text box will be left between the top of the object and the top of the element.

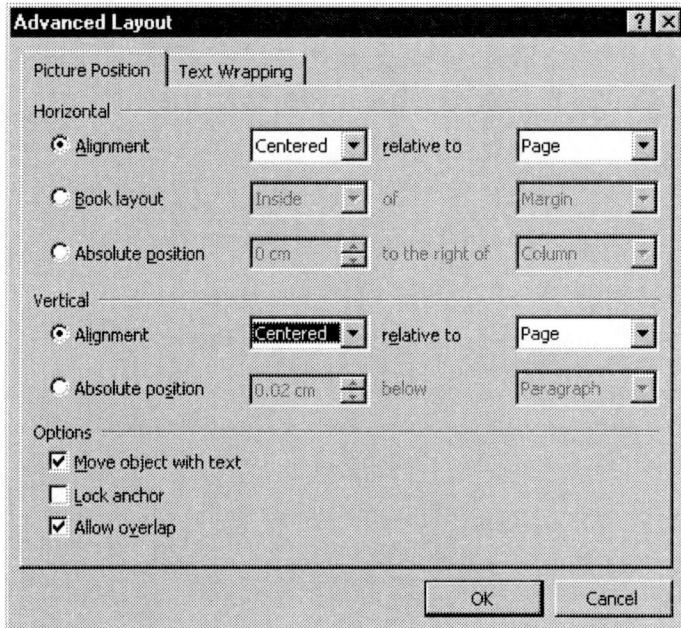

※ Set the attachment **Options** for the object:

Move object with text if this option is active, the object will move up or down with the text to which it is anchored.

Lock anchor activate this option to maintain the object's position in relation to the same paragraph; a padlock icon appears, indicating that the anchor position will remain the same even if the object is moved elsewhere.

Allow overlap if this option is active, objects that have the same wrapping style can be overlapped.

※ Click **OK** twice.

9 ▪ Sizing objects

- To change an object's size, select it (the small circles surrounding the object are called **handles**), then drag one of the selection handles.

- To resize several objects at once, select them using ⌷Shift⌷-clicks then drag one of the selection handles.

- To resize all the objects on a drawing canvas simultaneously, activate the drawing canvas in question.
  If the **Drawing Canvas** toolbar does not appear, display it by right-clicking the drawing canvas and choosing the **Show Drawing Canvas Toolbar** option. Click the **Scale Drawing** button on the **Drawing Canvas** toolbar. Drag one of the handles that appear on the canvas' hatched border. Click the **Scale Drawing** button to deactivate it.

- To resize the drawing canvas without changing the size of the objects it contains, activate the drawing canvas in question, then drag one of the thick black lines that appear just inside the hatched border.

  *You can also enlarge a drawing canvas by clicking, once or more depending on the required size, the **Expand** button on the **Drawing Canvas** toolbar.*

- To make a drawing canvas fit its contents, activate that drawing canvas then click the **Fit** button on the **Drawing Canvas** toolbar.

  This button only becomes available when the drawing canvas contains two or more items.

  📄 *To give an object an exact size, use the **Format** dialog box (**Format - last option on the menu - Size** tab).*

  ✎ *If you want to change an object's size without distorting its proportions, hold down ⌷Shift⌷ as you resize it.*

DOCUMENT CONTENTS AND PRESENTATION
Lesson 1.5: Drawing objects

📖 10 ▪ Changing an object's wrapping

▪ Select the object concerned.

You cannot change the wrapping of an object within a drawing canvas. However the drawing canvas itself is considered as an object so its wrapping can be changed.

▪ Choose the last option in the **Format** menu.

*The name of this option depends on the selected object: **Picture**, **Text Box**, **AutoShape** or **Drawing Canvas**.*

▪ Click the **Layout** tab.

▪ Choose a **Wrapping style** to define how the surrounding text will be positioned around the object.

▪ Specify the object's horizontal alignment in relation to the margins by using the options in the **Horizontal alignment** frame.

*The **Other** option aligns the object in accordance with what is defined in the **Advanced Layout** dialog box, which appears when you click the **Advanced** button.*

▪ You can make an even more precise choice by clicking the **Advanced** button then the **Text Wrapping** tab.

▪ If you wish, choose another **Wrapping style**.
In the **Wrap text** frame, indicate how the text should be distributed in relation to the object: on **Both sides**, on the **Left only**, on the **Right only** or **Largest only** (to place the text around the biggest side of the object).

*These options are only available for the **Square, Tight** and **Through** wrapping styles.*

▪ If necessary, use the **Distance from text** options to modify the distance separating the text from the sides of the object.

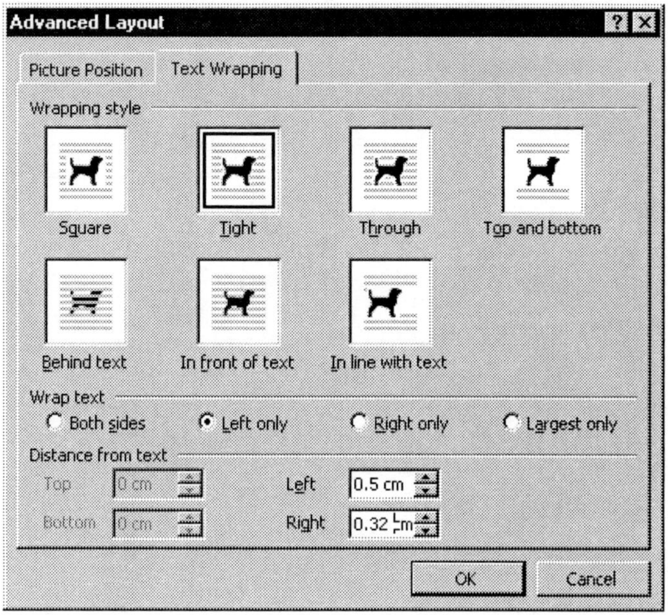

Advanced Layout dialog box — Text Wrapping tab showing Wrapping style options (Square, Tight, Through, Top and bottom, Behind text, In front of text, In line with text), Wrap text options (Both sides, Left only, Right only, Largest only), and Distance from text settings.

» Click **OK**.

*You return to the **Format** dialog box.*

» Click **OK**.

The 🖼 *tool button on the **Picture** and **Drawing Canvas** toolbars can also be used to change the wrapping style.*

📖 11 ▪ Moving objects

» To move an object, point to it (or if it is a text box, point to its edge) and when the pointer becomes a four-headed arrow, drag the object to its new position.

» To move several objects, select them with ⇧-clicks then point to one of the selected objects: when the pointer becomes a four-headed arrow, drag the group of objects to its new position.

▣ To move all the objects on a drawing canvas, activate the drawing canvas concerned, point to one of the edges of the frame surrounding it and when the pointer becomes a four-headed arrow, drag the drawing canvas to its new position.

📄 *If the **Snap objects to grid** option is active in the **Drawing Grid** dialog box (open the **Draw** list on the **Drawing** toolbar and take the **Grid** option), selected objects are attracted towards invisible gridlines on the page as you move them.*

12 ▪ Changing the stacking order of objects

▣ Select the object concerned.

▣ Open the **Draw** list on the **Drawing** toolbar and point to the **Order** option.

▣ Click one of the options given:

Bring to Front/   to make the object the first/last of all.
Send to Back

Bring Forward/   to move the object forward/backward one place.
Send Backward

13 ▪ Entering text in an object

▣ Right-click the object concerned.

▣ Click the **Add Text** option.

▣ Enter and format the text as usual.

▣ When you have finished, click outside the object.

The object is then considered as a text box.

📖 14 ▪ Changing an object's outline

▪ Select the object.

▪ Use the following tool buttons on the **Drawing** toolbar:

to change the colour of the outline or choose a repeated pattern to replace the line.

to change the line style and its thickness.

to change the type of line.

📖 15 ▪ Changing an object's background fill

Applying a colour

▪ Select the object.

▪ Open the list attached to the tool button then select the colour you want to apply to the object.

*The **More Fill Colors** option lets you select another colour or create your own custom colour.*

Applying a pattern or texture

▪ Select the object.

▪ Open the list attached to the tool button on the **Drawing** toolbar.

▪ Click the **Fill Effects** option.

※ Use one of the following tabs:

Gradient   applies **One color** or **Two colors** or **Preset** gradients, which may run in these directions: **Horizontal**, **Vertical**, **Diagonal up**, **Diagonal down**, **From corner** or **From center**.

Texture   applies a special textured fill effect.

Pattern   applies a **Pattern** using a **Foreground** and a **Background** colour.

Picture   fills the object with a picture.

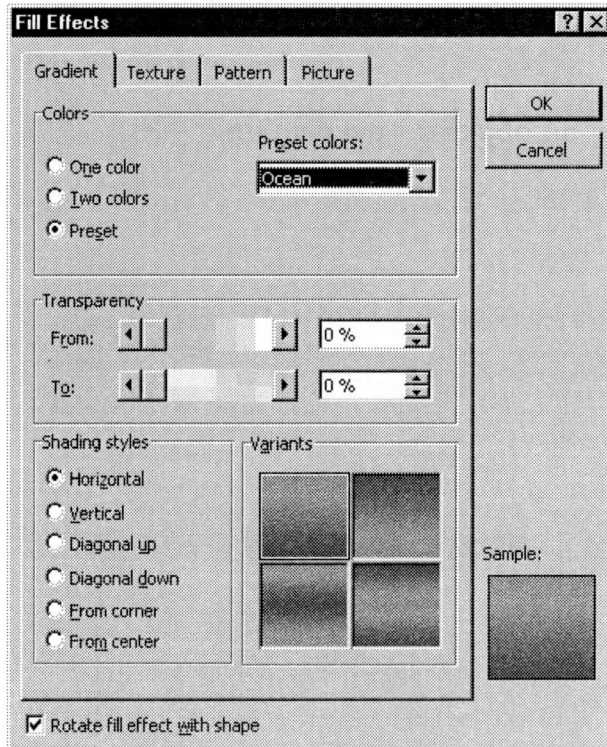

※ Click **OK**.

📄 *To remove an object's fill colour, open the list on the* 🔲 *tool button and choose the **No Fill** option.*

📖 16 ▪ Applying a shadow effect to an object

▪ Select the object.

▪ Click the 🔲 tool button on the **Drawing** toolbar.

▪ Click the required shadow effect.

*The **Shadow Settings** option allows you to customise the shadow (for example, you can change its colour).*

📖 17 ▪ Applying a 3D effect to an object

▪ Select the object.

▪ Click the 🔲 tool button on the **Drawing** toolbar.

▪ Click the required 3D effect.

The **No 3-D** option retrieves the original shape; the **3-D Settings** option provides further options to customise the effect.

Below, you can see **Practice Exercise** 1.5. This exercise is made up of 17 steps. If you do not know how to do one of the steps, go back to the title that corresponds to that particular lesson. When you have finished, you can check your work by reading the **Solution** that follows.

Steps in the exercise that are likely to be tested on the exam are preceded by this symbol: ▥. However, it is a good idea to complete all the steps in the exercise, to ensure that you have understood all the points discussed in the lesson.

☞ Practice Exercise 1.5

*To work on practice exercise 1.5, open the **1-5 Duty Roster.doc** document, located in the **MOUS Word 2002 Expert** folder.*

▥ 1. Using the **Insert Clip Art** task pane, find the clips that relate to **travel**, excluding those in the **Web Collections**. Insert the first clip in the second column of the list of pictures found into the first paragraph of the document (this is a picture of an aeroplane in a circle with a light blue background).
Finish by closing the **Insert Clip Art** task pane.

▥ 2. In the second cell of the first row in the table, insert the **Orbiting.wmf** picture, which is in the **MOUS Word 2002 Expert** folder.

▥ 3. In the third paragraph of the document, insert this WordArt object:

Westport Travel Shop

▥ 4. Modify the text of the WordArt object you just created to obtain this result:

Westport Travel

DOCUMENT CONTENTS AND PRESENTATION
Exercise 1.5: Drawing objects

5. Draw the objects shown in the example below. Draw them on a drawing canvas that you should insert in the fifth paragraph of the document; the rectangle should be approximately **3 cm** (1¼ in) wide and **1.5 cm** (¾ in) high, the star should be **8 cm** (3 in) wide and **5 cm** (2 in) high and the ellipse (oval) should be **1 cm** (½ in) wide and **4 cm** (1½ in) high. Draw the star using the AutoShape called **Explosion 1**.

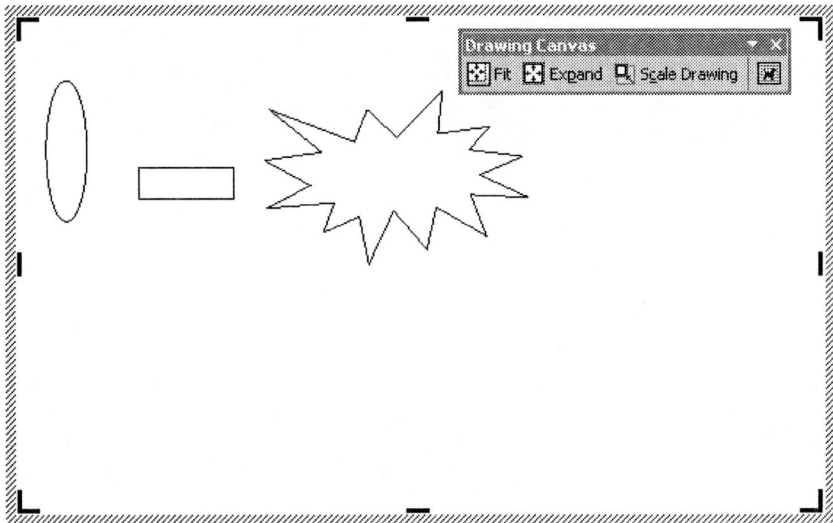

6. Select the rectangle and the star.

7. Delete the ellipse.

8. Position the top left corner of the rectangle in the drawing canvas at **4 cm** (1½ in) horizontally and **1 cm** (½ in) vertically.

9. Adjust the size of the drawing canvas to fit its contents. Change the size of the Clip Art picture (the plane in the circle) so it measures **3.5 cm** (1½ in) wide and **2.5 cm** (1 in) high.

10. Choose a **Behind text** wrapping style for the Clip Art picture (the plane), the WordArt object and the drawing canvas.

11. Move the objects created so far to obtain the following result:

12. Move the rectangle into the centre of the star then change the star's stacking order so it appears behind the rectangle. You should obtain the result shown below:

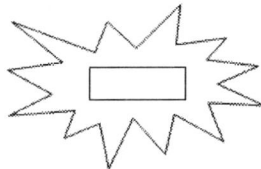

DOCUMENT CONTENTS AND PRESENTATION
Exercise 1.5: Drawing objects

Adjust the size of the drawing canvas so it fits its contents then move the drawing canvas to obtain the following result:

13. Enter the text **Travelling made easy** in the rectangle, centre this text horizontally and apply bold type to it:

14. Apply the **Sky Blue** colour and this line style: ═══ to the outline of the rectangle.

15. Apply the preset gradient called **Ocean** to the star object as its fill colour.

16. Apply a shadow effect of your own choice to the start shape.

17. Apply the 3D effect called **3-D Style 2** (the second 3D effect on the first row) to the star. Finish by closing and saving the changes made to the **1-5 Duty Roster.doc** document.

If you would like to practise these features more, on another document, you should work through Summary Exercise 1, on DOCUMENT CONTENTS AND PRESENTATION. You will find the summary exercises at the end of the book.

It is often possible to perform a task in several different ways, but here, only the easiest solution is presented. You can go back to the corresponding lesson if you want to see other techniques you could use.

Solution to Exercise 1.5

1. To use the Insert Clip Art task pane to find the clips that relate to "travel" except those in the Web Collections, start by using the **Insert - Picture - Clip Art** command to open the **Insert Clip Art** task pane.
   If the **Add Clips to Organizer** dialog box appears on the screen, click the **Now** button if you want to add the image, audio and video files from your hard disk into the Clip Organizer or, if you do not want to do that just yet, click the **Later** button
   Enter the keyword **travel** into the **Search text** box.
   Open the **Search in** list and make sure that the **Web Collections** check box is deactivated.
   Open the **Results should be** list and make sure that only the **Clip Art** option is ticked.
   Click the **Search** button to start the search.

   To insert the first clip in the second column of the list of pictures found into the first paragraph of the document, position the insertion point in the first paragraph of the **1-5 Duty Roster.doc** document then click the first picture in the second column of the **Results** list (this is the picture of an aeroplane in a circle with a light blue background).

   To close the **Insert Clip Art** task pane, click the ☒ button at the top right of the pane.

DOCUMENT CONTENTS AND PRESENTATION
Exercise 1.5: Drawing objects

▦ 2. To insert the **Orbiting.wmf** picture, which is in the **MOUS Word 2002 Expert** folder, which is in the second cell of the first row of the table, click the second cell in the table, and use the **Insert - Picture - From File** command.
If necessary, double-click the **MOUS Word 2002 Expert** folder.
Select the **Orbiting.wmf** image and click the **Insert** button.

▦ 3. To insert the WordArt object shown in step 3 into the third paragraph of the document, click the third paragraph. If the **Drawing** toolbar is not visible, show it by clicking the [⊞] tool button then click [◀].
Select the fourth WordArt effect in the first row then click **OK**.
Enter the text **Westport Travel Shop** then click **OK**.

▦ 4. To edit the WordArt text as shown in step 4, click the WordArt object to select it (if it is not already selected) and click the **Edit Text** button on the **WordArt** toolbar.
Select the word **Shop** then press the [Del] key. Click **OK**.

▦ 5. To draw the objects shown in step 5, on a drawing canvas inserted in the fifth paragraph of the document, start by displaying the **Drawing** toolbar with the [⊞] tool button (if the toolbar is not visible) then click the fifth paragraph of the document.

To draw the rectangle, click the [□] tool button then, inside the drawing canvas, drag to draw the rectangle, making it **3 cm** (1¼ in) wide and **1.5 cm** (¾ in) high.

To draw the star, open the **AutoShapes** list, point to the **Stars and Banners** category and choose the first shape (**Explosion 1**). Place the pointer inside the drawing canvas then drag to draw the star, making it **8 cm** (3 in) wide and **5 cm** (2 in) high.

To draw the ellipse, click the [○] tool button and drag to draw the ellipse, making it **1 cm** (½ in) wide and **4 cm** (1½ in) high.

6. To select the rectangle and the star, click the rectangle, hold down the `Shift` key and click the star.

7. To delete the ellipse, select it then press the `Del` key.

8. To position the top left corner of the rectangle in the drawing canvas at **4 cm** (1½ in) horizontally and **1 cm** (½ in) vertically, click the rectangle to select it, use the **Format - AutoShape** command then click the **Layout** tab. Enter **4 cm** in the **Horizontal** text box and **1 cm** in the **Vertical** text box. Make sure the **Top Left Corner** option is selected in the **From** list for both the **Horizontal** and **Vertical** options.
Click **OK**.

9. To adjust the size of the drawing canvas so it fits its contents, make sure the canvas is active (if not, select one of the objects within it to activate it). Click the **Fit** button on the **Drawing Canvas** toolbar.

   To change the size of the Clip Art picture (the plane in the circle) so it measures 3.5 cm (1½ in) wide and 2.5 cm (1 in) high, use `Ctrl` `Home` to go to the beginning of the document then click the picture to select it. Point to the bottom right handle and drag it until the picture is approximately **3.5 cm** (1½ in) wide and **2.5 cm** (1 in) high.

10. To apply a "Behind text" wrapping style to the Clip Art picture (the plane in the circle with the blue background), click the picture to select it. Use the **Format - Picture** command, click the **Layout** tab then click the **Behind text** option in the **Wrapping style** frame. Click **OK**.

   To apply a "Behind text" wrapping style to the WordArt object, click the WordArt object to select it. Use the **Format - WordArt** command, click the **Layout** tab then click the **Behind text** option in the **Wrapping style** frame. Click **OK**.

To apply a "Behind text" wrapping style to the drawing canvas, click under the rectangle to activate the drawing canvas (but make sure no object on the drawing canvas is actually selected). Use the **Format - Drawing Canvas** command, click the **Layout** tab then click the **Behind text** option in the **Wrapping style** frame. Click **OK**.

11. To move the WordArt object and the Clip Art picture as shown in step 11, point to the object concerned and when the pointer takes the shape of a four-headed arrow, drag the object to its new position.

To move the drawing canvas as shown in step 11, click under the rectangle to activate the drawing canvas (but make sure no object on the drawing canvas is actually selected). Point to one of the edges of the drawing canvas and when the pointer takes the shape of a four-headed arrow, drag the object to its new position.

12. To move the rectangle into the centre of the star as shown in step 12, point to the rectangle and when the pointer takes the shape of a four-headed arrow, drag the object to the centre of the star.

To change how the star overlaps so it appears behind the rectangle, click the star to select it and if it is not visible, display the **Drawing** toolbar by clicking the ![tool button] tool button. Open the **Draw** list on the **Drawing** toolbar, point to the **Order** option and choose the **Send to Back** option.

To adjust the size of the drawing canvas so it fits its contents, make sure the canvas is active and click the **Fit** button on the **Drawing Canvas** toolbar.

To move the drawing canvas as shown in step 12, click under the star so the canvas is active (but make sure none of the objects within it are selected). Point to one of the edges of the drawing canvas and when the pointer takes the shape of a four-headed arrow, drag the object to its new position.

13. To enter the text "Travelling made easy" in the rectangle, right-click the rectangle, click the **Add Text** option and type the text **Travelling made easy**.

To centre this text horizontally in the rectangle, click the [icon] tool button on the **Formatting** toolbar.

To apply bold type to this text, select the **Travelling made easy** text and click the **B** tool button on the **Formatting** toolbar.

14. To apply the colour Sky Blue to the outline of the rectangle, click the rectangle to select it, open the list on the [icon] tool button on the **Drawing** toolbar and click the **Sky Blue** colour.

To apply the ══════ line style to the outline of the rectangle, open the list on the [icon] tool button on the **Drawing** toolbar and click the second last style in the list.

15. To apply the preset gradient called "Ocean" to the star object as its fill colour, click the star to select it, open the list on the [icon] tool button on the **Drawing** toolbar, click the **Fill Effects** option then if necessary, click the **Gradient** tab.

Activate the **Preset** option in the **Colors** frame, select **Ocean** in the **Preset colors** list and click **OK**.

16. To apply a shadow effect of your choice to the star, click the star to select it.

Click the [icon] tool button on the **Drawing** toolbar to open its list and click the effect of your choice.

17. To apply the 3D effect called "3-D Style 2" to the star, click the star to select it, if it is not already selected.

Click the [icon] tool button on the **Drawing** toolbar to open its list and click the effect called **3-D Style 2** (the second 3D effect on the first row).

To close the **1-5 Duty Roster.doc** document, saving the changes made, use the **File - Close** command and click **Yes** on the message that asks if you want to save your changes before closing.

LONG DOCUMENTS
Lesson 2.1: Sections

1 ▪ Inserting a section break

A section is part of a document which has a particular layout (such as columns, a different orientation, specific headers and footers and so on). Before formatting sections, you must separate them with section breaks to differentiate them.

▪ Place the insertion point at the beginning of the new section you want to create.

▪ **Insert - Break**

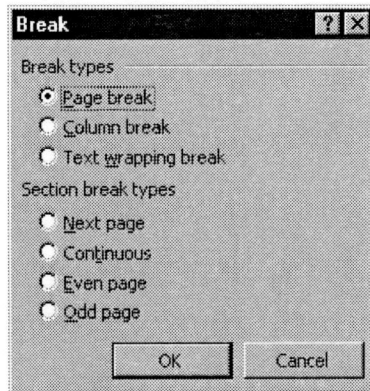

Break dialog box:

Break types
- ● Page break
- ○ Column break
- ○ Text wrapping break

Section break types
- ○ Next page
- ○ Continuous
- ○ Even page
- ○ Odd page

OK   Cancel

▪ Under **Section break types**, choose the type of separation you want between the sections:

Next page   inserts a section break that breaks the page, so the new section starts at the top of the page following the last page of the previous section.

Continuous   inserts a section break which starts the new section immediately after the previous one, without a page break.

Even page   inserts a section break and starts the new section on the next even-numbered page that occurs.

Odd page   inserts a section break and starts the new section on the next odd-numbered page that occurs.

▪ Click **OK**.

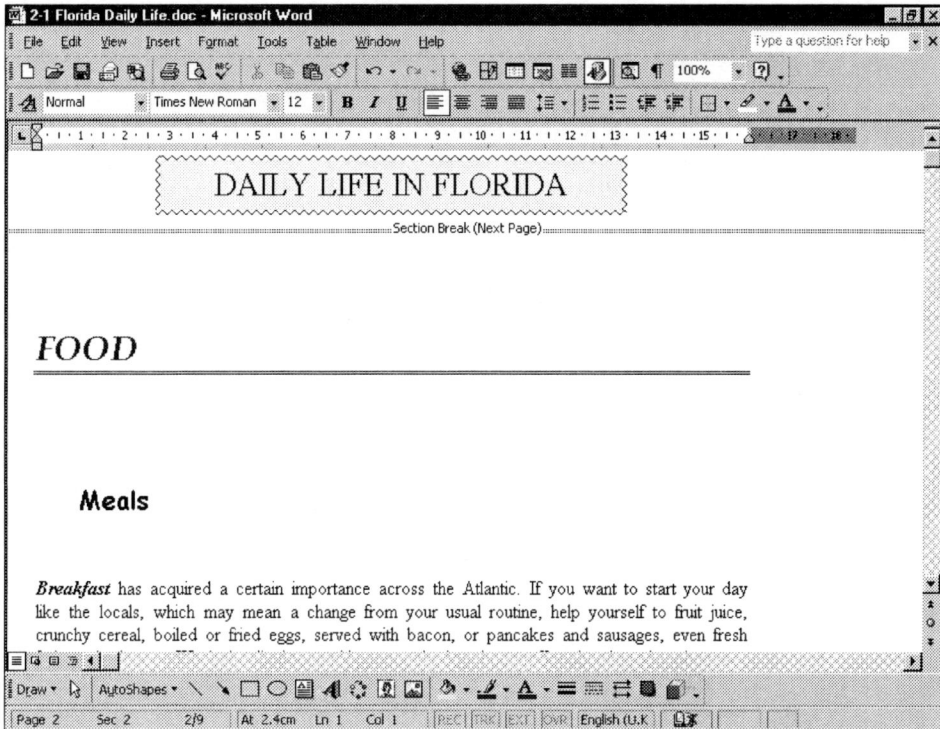

In Normal view, Word shows the break as a dotted line with the term **Section Break** followed by the type of break. The status bar gives the number of the new section.

2 • Formatting a section

- Place the insertion point in the section you want to format.

- Go to the required dialog box (**Page Setup, Borders and Shading, Columns** etc.) and make your presentation changes.

- In the **Apply to** list, choose **This section**.

- Click **OK**.

LONG DOCUMENTS
Exercise 2.1: Sections

Below, you can see **Practice Exercise** 2.1. This exercise is made up of 2 steps. If you do not know how to do one of the steps, go back to the title that corresponds to that particular lesson. When you have finished, you can check your work by reading the **Solution** that follows.

All the parts of this exercise are likely to be tested on the MOUS exam.

☞ Practice Exercise 2.1

*To work on practice exercise 2.1, open the **2-1 Florida Daily Life.doc** document, located in the **MOUS Word 2002 Expert** folder.*

1. Insert a section break that will create a page break in the empty paragraph following the **DAILY LIFE IN FLORIDA** title on the first page of the document.

2. Apply a **Landscape** presentation to the first section of the document and close the document, saving the changes made.

If you would like to practise these features more, on another document, you should work through Summary Exercise 2, on LONG DOCUMENTS. You will find the summary exercises at the end of the book.

It is often possible to perform a task in several different ways, but here, only the easiest solution is presented. You can go back to the corresponding lesson if you want to see other techniques you could use.

Solution to Exercise 2.1

1. To insert a section break, which will also start a new page, in the empty paragraph that follows the DAILY LIFE IN FLORIDA title at the top of the document, start by clicking the empty paragraph in question.
Use the **Insert - Break** command and in the **Section break types** frame, click the **Next page** option.
Click **OK**.

2. To apply a landscape page orientation to the document's first section, place the insertion point inside that section (for example, on the DAILY LIFE IN FLORIDA title).
Use the **File - Page Setup** command then if necessary, click the **Margins** tab.
Click the **Landscape** option then if necessary, choose **This section** in the **Apply to** drop-down list.
Click **OK**.

To close the document and save the changes made, use the **File - Close** command then click the **Yes** button on the message that asks you if you want to save your changes.

LONG DOCUMENTS
Exercise 2.1: Sections

LONG DOCUMENTS
Lesson 2.2: Notes and bookmarks

1 ▪ Creating footnotes and endnotes

Footnotes and endnotes are ways of adding explanations, comments and references relative to the main text of your document.

▪ Position the insertion point where you wish to insert the note reference.

▪ **Insert - Reference - Footnote**

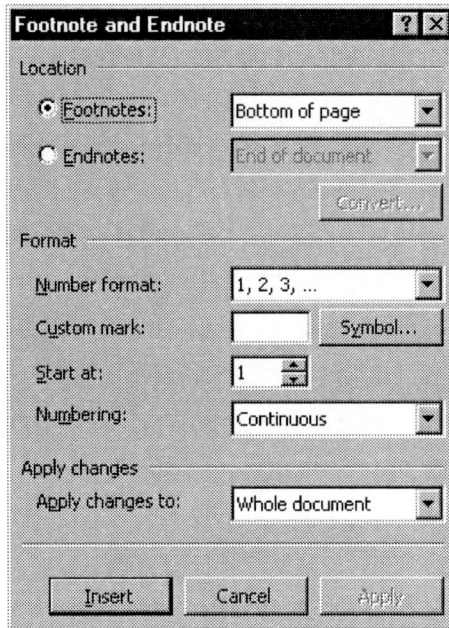

▪ Specify what sort of note you are creating by choosing **Footnotes** or **Endnotes** in the **Location** frame.

- Indicate where the note should be printed, using the drop-down list on **Footnotes** or **Endnotes**, whichever is active:

	Position	Notes are printed
For footnotes	**Bottom of page**	above the bottom margin
	Below text	under the last line of text
For endnotes	**End of section**	after the section
	End of document	at the end of the document

- If you want the notes to be numbered automatically, use the **Number format** list to change the way numbers look.

  When automatic numbering is in place, Word updates the numbers when you add, move or delete notes.

- If you want to create your own note reference, click the text box on the **Custom mark** option and enter the note reference (up to 10 characters) or click the **Symbol** button to choose a symbol as the reference.

  *The **Number format** and **Start at** options become unavailable when you create a custom reference.*

- When automatic numbering is in place, you can enter a new number or character by which to start numbering in the **Start at** box.

- Open the **Numbering** list to specify whether numbering should be **Continuous** throughout the document, or should it **Restart each section** or **Restart each page**.

- Click the **Insert** button.

  In Normal view, the insertion point appears in the note pane at the bottom of the window.
  In Print Layout view, the insertion point appears at the bottom of the page above the footer. A line separates the text area from the note area.

- Enter the text of the note.

LONG DOCUMENTS
Lesson 2.2: Notes and bookmarks

The style reserved for the text of a note is called "Footnote text " or "Endnote text " and the one for the marks referring to the note is called "Footnote (or Endnote) reference ".

» Click inside the document or press F6 if you are in Normal view.

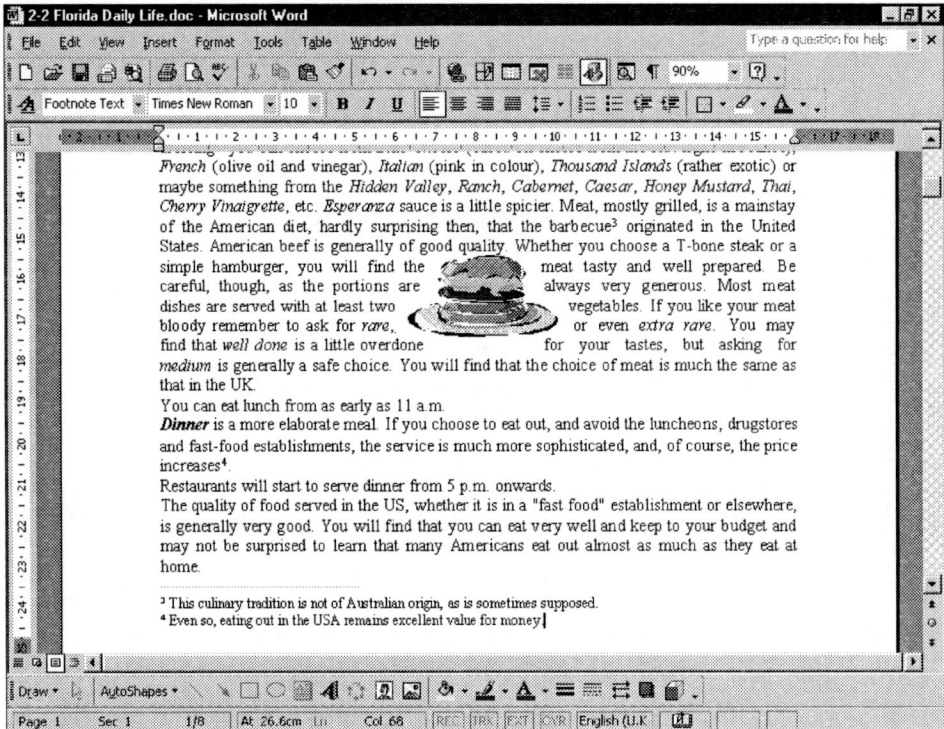

» To see the content of a note, point to its reference (without clicking) or, if you are in Normal view, use the note pane (cf. Using the note pane).

*When you point to a reference, the content of the note appears in a ScreenTip, providing the **ScreenTips** option is active in **Tools - Options - View** tab.*

📄 *The **Convert** button on the **Footnote and Endnote** dialog box (**Insert - Reference - Footnote**) converts a footnote into an endnote and vice versa.*

Word keeps space at the end of the page so that footnote contents are always printed on the same page as their reference.

*To move from note to note, click the **Select Browse Object** button (◉) on the vertical scroll bar then the 🔲 button or the 🔲 button to browse respectively the endnotes or footnotes.*

2 ▪ Using the note pane

▪ **View - Normal**

▪ To open the note pane, while in Normal view, activate the **Footnotes** option in the **View** menu or double-click the note reference.

▪ To alter the height of the note pane, drag the top edge of the pane.

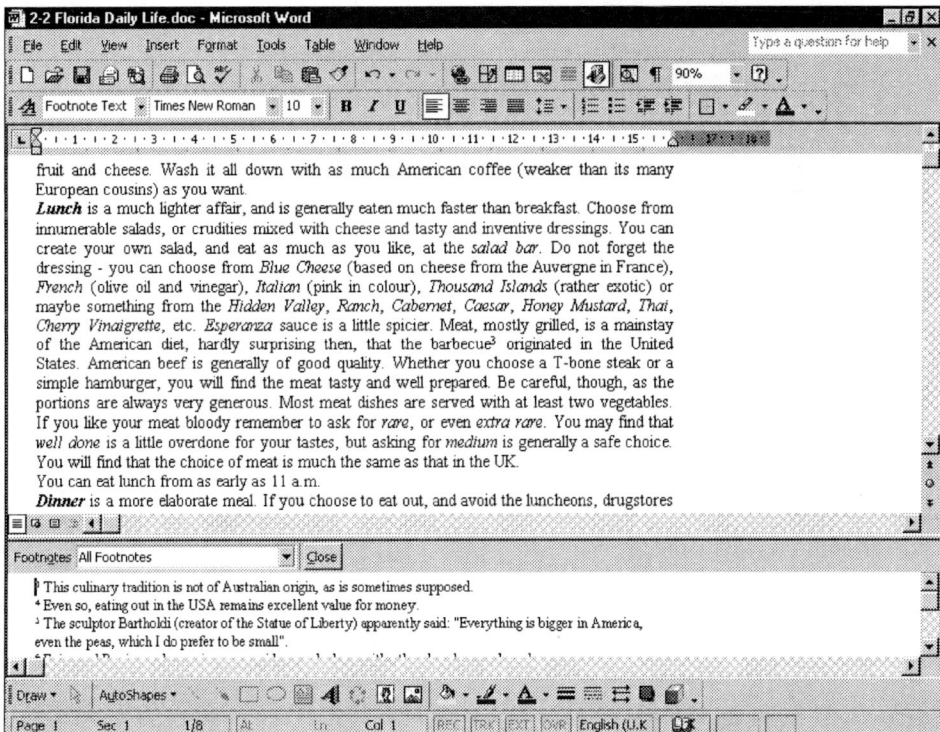

* To reach a note reference quickly, click the text of the corresponding footnote or endnote then click the reference in the text.

* To close the note pane, deactivate the **Footnotes** option in the **View** menu or click the **Close** button on the note pane.

3 ▪ Managing existing notes

To manage notes, you need to work on the note reference and not the text of the note.

* To change a note's contents while in Print Layout view, double-click the note reference and make your changes.

* To delete a note, select the note reference and press Del.

* To move a note, move the note reference as you would a normal piece of text.

📄 *If automatic numbering is active, the notes are then renumbered automatically.*

4 ▪ Modifying the format and/or the position of notes

* Place the mouse pointer anywhere in the document.

* **Insert - Reference - Footnote**

* Make your changes in the **Format** and/or **Location** frames.

* Open the **Apply changes to** list and click the option corresponding to the part of the document in which you want to apply your modifications.

* Click the **Apply** button.

5 ▪ Using the Document Map

▪ **View - Document Map** or ▨

*A grey pane, called the **Document Map** or the **Document Navigator** appears at the left of the screen. It displays an outline of the document.*

▪ In the Document Map, click the part of the document you want to reach.

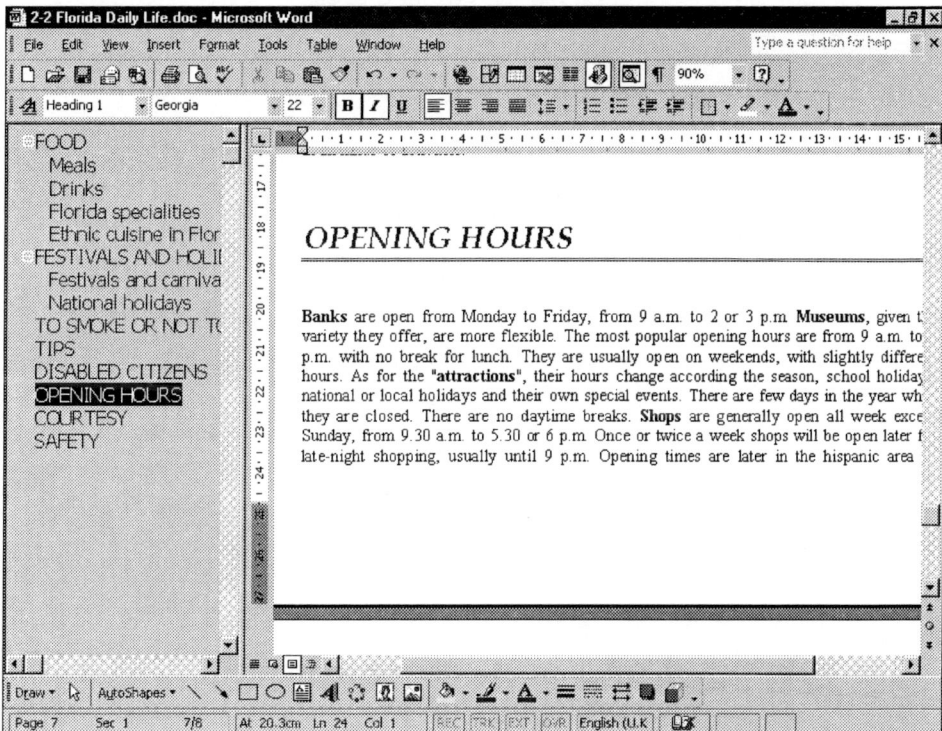

The chosen part of the document appears immediately in the right pane.

▪ Click the ▨ tool button again to deactivate the Document Map.

▤6 ▪ Working with bookmarks

A bookmark allows you to mark a place in a text so that you can find it immediately.

Creating a bookmark

▪ If going to the bookmark should also involve selecting a passage of text, select that text. If going to the bookmark is simply a matter of moving the insertion point, put the insertion point in the required position.

▪ **Insert - Bookmark** or `Ctrl` `Shift` `F5`

▪ Enter the **Bookmark name** in the corresponding box.

A bookmark name can contain up to 40 characters; it must start with a letter and must not contain any spaces.

▪ Click the **Add** button.

Deleting a bookmark

▪ **Insert - Bookmark** or `Ctrl` `Shift` `F5`

▪ In the **Bookmark name** list box, select the bookmark you want to delete.

▪ Click the **Delete** button then click **Close**.

Using a bookmark

▪ **Insert - Bookmark** or `Ctrl` `Shift` `F5`

▪ If required, in **Sort by**, choose to sort the bookmark list by the **Location** of the bookmark in the document or by its **Name**.

▪ Tick the **Hidden bookmarks** option to show any hidden bookmarks (or deactivate this option to keep them hidden).

▪ Double-click the bookmark you want to go to or select it and click the **Go To** button.

* Shut the dialog box using the **Close** button.

> *Bookmarks can also be reached with the **Edit - Go To** command or* `Ctrl` *G.*

7 ▪ Creating cross-references

A cross-reference refers to an item (a title, a footnote, a bookmark, a caption etc.) which is in another place in the document.

* At the required place in the document, type the introductory text for the cross-reference.

* **Insert - Reference - Cross-reference**

* In the **Reference type** list, choose the type of item to which the cross-reference will refer.

* In the **Insert reference to** list, select the information that will be shown in the cross-reference (such as a page number).

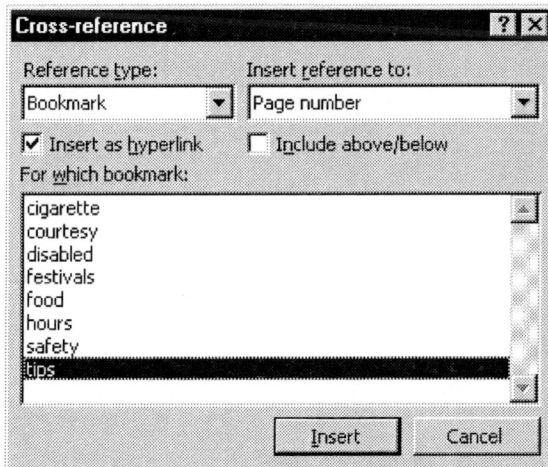

The contents of this list depend on the selected reference type.

- In the **For which (object name)** list, select the item to which the cross-reference will refer.

- Make sure the **Insert as hyperlink** option is ticked if you want to go to the item mentioned when you click the cross-reference.

- Activate the **Include above/below** option if you want to add the words **above** or **below** to the cross-reference (this corresponds to its position in relation to the associated item).

- Click the **Insert** button.

- If required, define all the other cross-references needed.

- Close the **Cross-reference** dialog box by clicking its **Close** button.

> To change the item referred to by a cross-reference, select the cross-reference concerned then go into the **Cross-reference** dialog box (**Insert - Reference - Cross-reference**) and click the new item in the **Insert reference to** list.
>
> To update the cross-references, select either the cross-reference concerned or the entire document to update all then right-click the selection and click the **Update Fields** option.

Below, you can see **Practice Exercise** 2.2. This exercise is made up of 7 steps. If you do not know how to do one of the steps, go back to the title that corresponds to that particular lesson. When you have finished, you can check your work by reading the **Solution** that follows.

Steps in the exercise that are likely to be tested on the exam are preceded by this symbol: ⊞. However, it is a good idea to complete all the steps in the exercise, to ensure that you have understood all the points discussed in the lesson.

☞ Practice Exercise 2.2

To work on practice exercise 2.2, open the **2-2 Florida Daily Life.doc** document, located in the **MOUS Word 2002 Expert** folder.

⊞ 1. Create the footnotes shown in the table below, following these guidelines:

- the notes should print beneath the text,

- the notes should be numbered automatically and the number format should be **1, 2, 3 ...**,

- Word should starting numbering the notes at 3,

- the note numbering should be continuous throughout the document.

Text concerned	Footnote content
barbecue (page 1)	This culinary tradition is not of Australian origin, as is sometimes supposed.
the price increases (page 1)	Even so, eating out in the USA remains excellent value for money.

2. Open the note pane, go to the reference for note **5** then close the note pane. Activate **Print Layout** view.

3. Move the marker for note **5** after the word **Europe** in the same sentence then delete note **7** (page 4).

4. Change the place where the notes are printed so they now print at the bottom of each page containing note references then ask Word to start numbering at **1**.

5. Using the Document Map, go to the **OPENING HOURS** title in the document. When you have finished, close the Document Map pane.

6. Create a bookmark called **hours** that will place the insertion point in front of the **OPENING HOURS** title on page **7**.
Delete the **sandwich** bookmark then go to the text that talks about courtesy with the bookmark called **courtesy**.

7. After the **Restaurants will start to serve dinner from 5 p.m. onwards** text (page 1) create a cross-reference that will refer to the **tips** bookmark. The introductory text for the cross-reference should read **See also TIPS on page** `Space`; the information you want to insert in the document is the **Page Number** and a click on the cross-reference should take you to the **tips** bookmark.
To finish, save the changes and close the document.

If you would like to practise these features more, on another document, you should work through Summary Exercise 2, on LONG DOCUMENTS. You will find the summary exercises at the end of the book.

It is often possible to perform a task in several different ways, but here, only the easiest solution is presented. You can go back to the corresponding lesson if you want to see other techniques you could use.

Solution to Exercise 2.2

1. To create the first footnote described in step 1, click after the word "barbecue" on page 1 then use the **Insert - Reference - Footnote** command.

   Leave the **Footnotes** option active then open the drop-down list next to this option and select **Below text**, which will print the notes beneath the last line of each page concerned. To activate automatic numbering and give a 1, 2, 3... format to the numbers, make sure the **1, 2, 3, ...** option is selected in the **Number format** list.

   So that Word starts numbering the notes at 3, type **3** in the **Start at** text box.

   To ensure the note numbering is continuous throughout the document make sure the **Continuous** option is selected in the **Numbering** list box. Click the **Insert** button then enter the text **This culinary tradition is not of Australian origin, as is sometimes supposed**.

   To create the second footnote described in step 1, click after the text "the price increases" on page 1 then use the **Insert - Reference - Footnote** command.

   Leave the options as they are in the **Footnote and Endnote** dialog box and click the **Insert** button.

   Enter the text **Even so, eating out in the USA remains excellent value for money.**

2. To open the note pane, use the **View - Normal** command then use **View - Footnotes**.

   To go to the reference for note 5, click the text of note **5** in the note pane then click the note reference in the document.

To close the note pane, click the **Close** button that appears within it.

To activate **Print Layout** view, use the **View - Print Layout** command.

3. To move the marker for note 5 after the word "Europe" in the same sentence, select the reference for note **5**.

Click the [✂] tool button, click after the word **Europe** then click the [📋] tool button.

To delete note 7, select the note reference **7** (page 4) then press the [Del] key.

4. To change the place where the notes are printed so they now print at the bottom of each page containing note references, activate the **Insert - Reference - Footnote** command.
Open the list on the **Footnotes** option and click the **Bottom of page** option.
To start the note numbering at 1, enter **1** in the **Start at** text box.
Click the **Apply** button to finish.

5. To use the Document Map to go to the OPENING HOURS title, start by opening the Document Map by clicking the [🔍] tool button on the **Standard** toolbar.
Next, click the **OPENING HOURS** title on the Document Map pane.

To close the Document Map, deactivate the [🔍] tool button by clicking it again.

6. To create the bookmark called "hours", click before the **OPENING HOURS** title on page 7 and use the **Insert - Bookmark** command.
Enter **hours** in the **Bookmark name** text box and click the **Add** button.

To delete the "sandwich" bookmark, use **Insert - Bookmark**, select the **sandwich** bookmark then click the **Delete** button then **Close**.

To go to the text that talks about courtesy, activate the **Insert - Bookmark** command, double-click the **courtesy** bookmark then click the **Close** button.

7. To create a cross-reference referring to the "tips" bookmark, click after the "Restaurants will start to serve dinner from 5 p.m. onwards" text (page 1), press the `Space` key and enter **See also TIPS on page** `Space`.
   Use the **Insert - Reference - Cross-reference** command, select **Bookmark** in the **Reference type** list and **Page number** in the **Insert reference to** list.
   In the **For which bookmark** list, select **tips**, leave the **Insert as hyperlink** option active and click **Insert** then **Close**.

To save the changes made to the document, click the tool button.

Close the document with the **File - Close** command.

LONG DOCUMENTS
Lesson 2.3: Outlines and tables

1 ▪ Creating an outline using preset styles

▪ Activate **Outline** view using the **View - Outline** command or [icon].

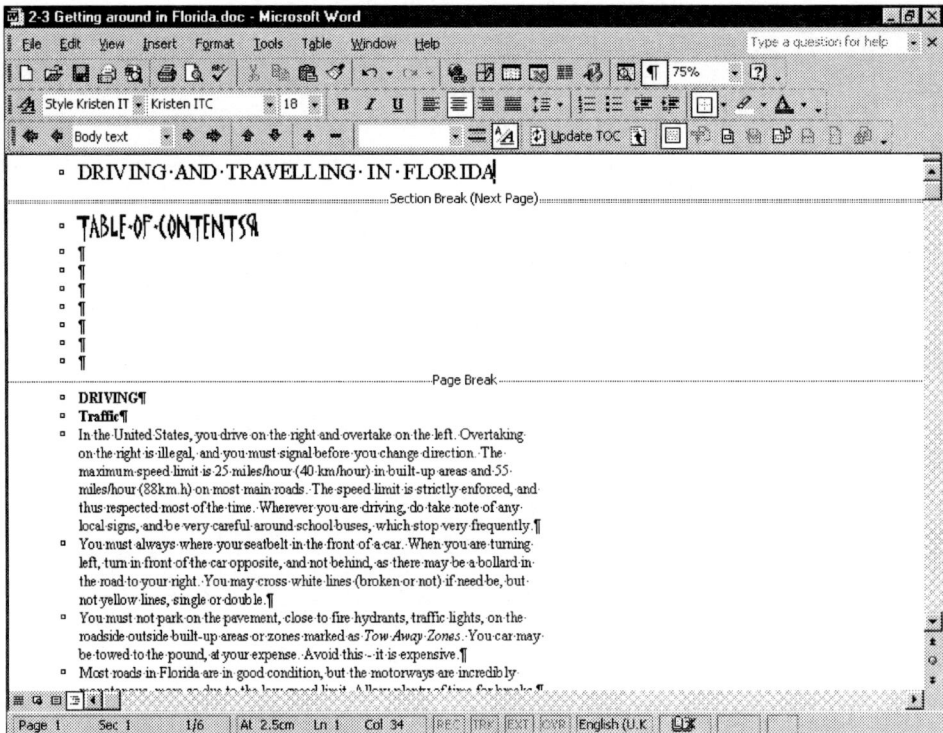

```
2-3 Getting around in Florida.doc - Microsoft Word
File  Edit  View  Insert  Format  Tools  Table  Window  Help          Type a question for help

Style Kristen IT   Kristen ITC      18    B  I  U
Body text                                Update TOC

      □   DRIVING·AND·TRAVELLING·IN·FLORIDA
                          Section Break (Next Page)
      □   TABLE·OF·CONTENTS¶
      □   ¶
      □   ¶
      □   ¶
      □   ¶
      □   ¶
      □   ¶
                             Page Break
      □   DRIVING¶
      □   Traffic¶
      □   In·the·United·States,·you·drive·on·the·right·and·overtake·on·the·left.·Overtaking·
          on·the·right·is·illegal,·and·you·must·signal·before·you·change·direction.·The·
          maximum·speed·limit·is·25·miles/hour·(40·km/hour)·in·built-up·areas·and·55·
          miles/hour·(88km.h)·on·most·main·roads.·The·speed·limit·is·strictly·enforced,·and·
          thus·respected·most·of·the·time.·Wherever·you·are·driving,·do·take·note·of·any·
          local·signs,·and·be·very·careful·around·school·buses,·which·stop·very·frequently.¶
      □   You·must·always·where·your·seatbelt·in·the·front·of·a·car.·When·you·are·turning·
          left,·turn·in·front·of·the·car·opposite,·and·not·behind,·as·there·may·be·a·bollard·in·
          the·road·to·your·right.·You·may·cross·white·lines·(broken·or·not)·if·need·be,·but·
          not·yellow·lines,·single·or·double.¶
      □   You·must·not·park·on·the·pavement,·close·to·fire·hydrants,·traffic·lights,·on·the·
          roadside·outside·built-up·areas·or·zones·marked·as·Tow·Away·Zones.·You·car·may·
          be·towed·to·the·pound,·at·your·expense.·Avoid·this·-·it·is·expensive.¶
      □   Most·roads·in·Florida·are·in·good·condition,·but·the·motorways·are·incredibly·

Page 1    Sec 1    1/6    At 2.5cm  Ln 1   Col 34        English (U.K
```

The Outlining bar replaces the ruler and each paragraph is preceded by an empty square.

▪ To enter a heading in an outline, apply preset styles according to the importance of the heading:

Heading 1   principal headings,

Heading 2   subheadings,

Heading 3   sub-subheadings.

*Nine preset heading styles are available but only three appear in the **Styles** list. To see all of them, display the **Styles and Formatting** task pane then click the **All styles** option in the **Show** list.*

*You can apply preset styles in other views than Outline view. The **Heading 1**, **Heading 2** and **Heading 3** styles remove your own formatting. You can however customise these styles by applying your own formatting subsequently. A cross to the left of a text indicates that this will appear as a heading in an outline.*

- Once you have entered the heading in the plan, you can promote it to a higher importance level with the ⬅ button or demote it with the ➡ button.

📄 *If a normal text has been defined as a heading by accident, you can undo this by applying a style other than **Heading 1**, **Heading 2**, **Heading 3**, etc.*

Leave Outline view by choosing a different view.

If certain paragraphs in your document contain custom styles that you do not want to replace with preset styles, you will have to apply an outline level to each style when you create a document outline (cf. following section).

2 ▪ Assigning outline levels to paragraphs/styles

If you want to create a table of contents or number your headings automatically, but do not want to lose your custom formatting, you need to apply an outline level to all your paragraphs or paragraph styles.

To a paragraph

- Place the insertion point in the paragraph concerned or select that paragraph.
- **Format - Paragraph - Indents and Spacing** tab
- In the **Outline level** list, choose the level (from 1 to 9) that you want to apply to the paragraph.
- Click **OK**.

* Define the outline level for each paragraph in the same way.

To a paragraph style

* Make sure the insertion point is not in a paragraph containing a preset heading style (Heading1, Heading2 and so on).

* Show the **Styles and Formatting** toolbar by clicking the ⊞ tool button on the **Formatting** toolbar.

* In the **Pick formatting to apply** list, point to the style to which you want to assign an outline level, then click the ▾ button and choose the **Modify Style** option.

* Click the **Format** list and choose the **Paragraph** option.

* In the **Outline level** list, choose the level (from 1 to 9) that you want to assign to that paragraph style.

* Click **OK** twice.

3 ▪ Using a document outline

* Go into Outline view with the **View - Outline** command.

* To display the headings of a particular level and above, open the **Show Level** list `Show Level 4 ▾`. For example, if you click **Show Level 3**, you will see all the Level 3 headings as well as those for levels 1 and 2.

   You can also select a level by holding down `Alt` and `Shift` and typing the level's number on the alphanumerical keyboard.

```
  ° DRIVING¶
      ° Traffic¶
      ° Signs¶
      ° If·you·break·down¶
  ° TRANSPORT¶
      ° By·air¶
      ° By·road¶
          ° Hire·cars¶
              ° Conditions¶
              ° Details¶
              ° Hiring·a·car¶
          ° Chauffeur·driven·cars¶
          ° Motorbikes¶
          ° Coaches¶
      ° By·train¶
```

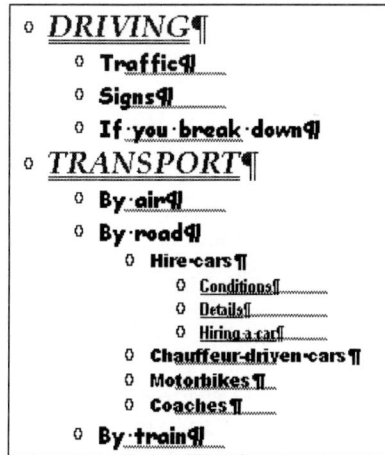

* To view the whole document (headings and text), open the **Show Level** list `Show Level 4  ▾` and click the **Show All Levels** option.

* To hide the text linked to the active heading, double-click the cross that precedes the heading or click the [▬] tool button or press the - (minus) key on the number pad.

* To show the text linked to the active heading, double-click the cross that precedes the heading or click the [✚] tool button or press the + (plus) key on the number pad.

* To promote a heading up one level, place the insertion point in the heading concerned, then click the [◈] tool button or press [Alt][Shift][←].

* To demote a heading down one level, place the insertion point in the heading concerned, then click the [◈] tool button or press [Alt][Shift][→].

* To move a heading with any associated text or subheadings, point to the cross that precedes the heading then drag it to its new position or click the title then the [⬆] or [⬇] tool button.

* To print a document outline, show only the headings then start printing.

The print preview shows the whole document, but only the outline's headings will actually be printed.

4 ▪ Creating a table of contents from an outline

▪ Place the insertion point where you want to insert the table of contents.

▪ **Insert - Reference - Index and Tables**

▪ Click the **Table of Contents** tab.

▪ In the **Formats** list in the **General** frame, choose the presentation you want to apply to the table of contents. You can check the result in the **Print Preview** frame. To create a custom presentation, select the **From template** option and click the **Modify** button.

You can also see a Web Preview of your table of contents, showing how it would appear in a Web browser.

▪ If you wish, indicate what items you wish to display and how that should be done: do you wish to **Show page numbers**? If so, do you want to **Right align page numbers**?

▪ For all the **Formats** except **Simple** and **Modern**, indicate whether you wish to add a **Tab leader** between the headings and the page numbers.

▪ Using the **Show levels** list, give the number of heading levels that should appear in the table of contents.

Index and Tables ? X

| Index | Table of Contents | Table of Figures | Table of Authorities |

Print Preview

HEADING 1............................. 1

  HEADING 2............................ 3

    Heading 3 5

      Heading 4............................7

Web Preview

HEADING 1

  HEADING 2

    Heading 3

      Heading 4

☑ Show page numbers

☑ Right align page numbers

Tab leader: |........ ▼|

☑ Use hyperlinks instead of page numbers

General

Formats: |Formal ▼| Show levels: |4 ⬍|

[Show Outlining Toolbar]   [Options...] [Modify...]

[OK] [Cancel]

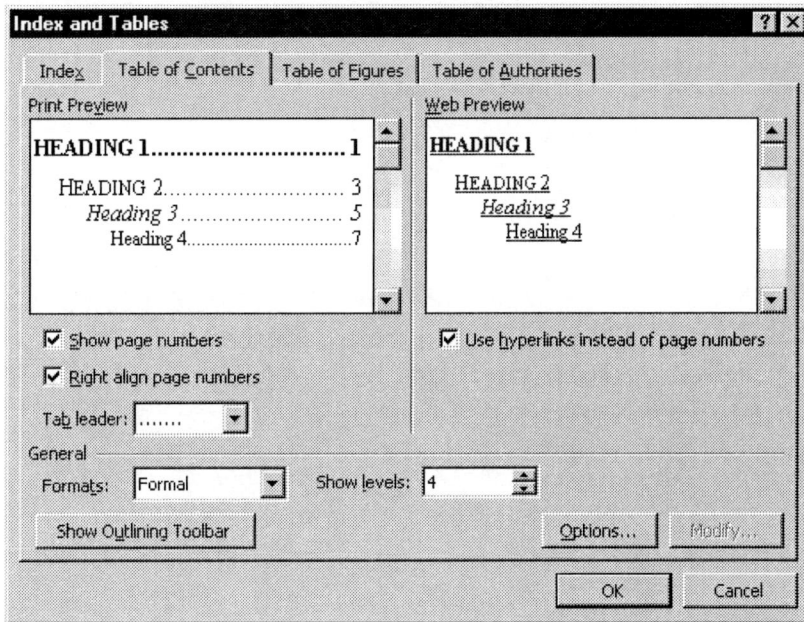

- ⁂ If you intend to display your table of contents in a Web browser and you want a hyperlink to be created for each heading, make sure the **Use hyperlinks instead of page numbers** option is active.

  When this option is active, hyperlinks are created for each title in the table of contents inserted in the document, without removing the page numbers.

- ⁂ If you want to see the **Outlining** toolbar in the document, click the **Show Outlining Toolbar** button.

- ⁂ Click **OK**.

- ⁂ If required, use ⌐Alt⌐F9 to hide the code corresponding to the table of contents and view the entries it contains.

  *If the **Use hyperlinks instead of page numbers** option is active in the **Index and Tables** dialog box (**Table of Contents** tab), a hyperlink will be created for each title in the table.*

▪ To go to a heading in the document, hold down the ⌷Ctrl⌷ key and click the corresponding title in the table of contents.

📄 *When you select the table of contents, it appears with a grey background. You can choose to display this background permanently (or never at all) using the **Field shading** option in the **Options** dialog box (**Tools - Options - View** tab).*

*To change how the table of contents is presented, select another format in the **Table of Contents** page of the **Index and Tables** dialog box (**Insert - Reference - Index and Tables**). Once you have confirmed your choice, the new presentation replaces the old one.*

*The ⌷↑⌷ tool button on the **Outlining** toolbar selects the table of contents no matter where the insertion point is in the document.*

▦5 ▪ Updating a table of contents

▪ Click one of the titles in the table of contents to activate it.

The grey background indicates that the table of contents is active.

▪ Press the ⌷F9⌷ key or the ⌷Update TOC⌷ button on the **Outlining** toolbar.

▪ Choose whether to **Update page numbers only** or to **Update entire table**.

▪ Click **OK**.

6 ▪ Creating an index

Here is an example of the type of index you might draw up:

B		M	

Break down 4		Motorbike
		  Hire 6
		Motoribike
		  Travelling 6	

C		**P**	

Car
  Chauffeur driven 6
  Cost........... 6
  Fuel........... 6
  Hire car conditions 5
  Hire car details 5
  How to hire a car 5
Cars
  American cars 4
Coach
  Travelling 6
Cost
  Hire car 6
		Petrol
		  Car 6
		Plane 7	

D		**R**	

Driving
  American cars 4
  Breaking down 4
  Signs 3
  Traffic 3
		Road
		  Transport 5	

		S	

		Signs
		  Junctions 3
		  Urban roads......... 3
		Speed
		  Traffic 3	

Defining an index entry

▪ If the entry exists already, select it; otherwise place the insertion point where the subject of the index entry is.

▪ **Insertion - Reference - Index and Tables - Index** tab - **Mark Entry** button or Alt Shift X

▪ If necessary, click the **Main entry** box and type in the corresponding entry.

▪ Go to the **Subentry** box and if required type the index subentry.

* If other entry levels need to be created, type a colon (:) before entering the rest of the text in the **Subentry** box.

* Activate the **Cross-reference** option if you want to add a cross-reference to the index rather than a page number.

* Activate the **Current page** option to show the number of the page containing the selected index entry.

   This option is active by default.

* Activate the **Page range** option to select, in the **Bookmark** list, the bookmark that signals the end of the page range for the entry.

* If you wish to apply **Bold** or **Italic** type to the page numbers given to that index entry, tick the corresponding **Page number format** option.

* If required, use shortcut keys to format the characters entered.

* Confirm by clicking **Mark** then click the **Close** button.

   If the nonprinting characters are visible, you will be able to see the inserted field codes {XE...}.

Inserting an index table

* Place the insertion point where you want the index to appear.

* **Insert - Reference - Index and Tables**

* Click the **Index** tab, if necessary.

* Choose a look for the subentries under **Type**:

Indented   the subentries are indented in relation to the main entries and are placed one beneath the other.

Run-in   the entries are listed one beneath the other but the subentries are listed side by side, separated by semi-colons.

* In the **Formats** list, select the option that corresponds to the presentation you want the index to have and view the result in the **Print Preview** frame. To create a custom presentation, select the **From template** option and click the **Modify** button.

* If it is possible, and if required, choose to **Right align page numbers**, add a **Tab leader**, place the index in two or more **Columns** or choose a **Language** for the index.

* Click **OK**.

> The styles used in the table are called **Index 1**, **Index 2** and so on and can be modified.
>
> When you select an index, as with a table of contents, it appears with a grey background. You can choose to display this background permanently (or never at all) using the **Field shading** option in the **Options** dialog box (**Tools - Options - View** tab).

7 ▪ Updating an index

* Click inside the index table.

* Press the F9 key.

▣8 ▪ Creating a table of figures

A table of figures shows the list of the captions on all the pictures, drawings, objects and any other illustrations contained within the document.

Associating a caption with an object

▪ Select the object concerned (picture, drawing, table etc.); if you want the caption to be included subsequently in the table of figures, you must ensure its **Wrapping style** is **In line with text** (to modify this option, open the **Format** menu, take the last option and click the **Layout** tab).

▪ **Insert - Reference - Caption**

▪ In the **Label** box, choose the type of label for the object (**Equation**, **Figure** or **Table**) or click the **New Label** button to create your own label.

If you choose this last option, the new label will appear in the Caption text box.

▪ In the **Caption** box, make any necessary changes to the text displayed.

▪ In the **Position** box, select the option that describes where you want the caption to go: **Below selected item** or **Above selected item**.

▪ If you wish, click the **Numbering** button, open the **Format** list box and select the number format you want to apply. Click **OK**.

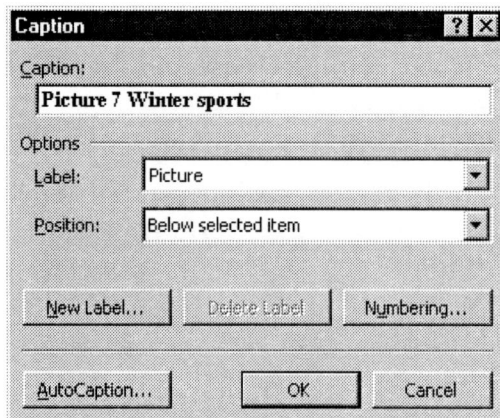

» Click **OK** to insert the caption.

📄 *If you click the **AutoCaption** button on this dialog box, you can add captions automatically: you choose the type of object to which captions should be applied and each time this type of object is inserted, the caption appears. You should activate this feature when you first create your document, before inserting any objects.*

Inserting a table of figures

» Place the insertion point where you want the table of figures to appear.

» **Insert - Reference - Index and Tables**

» Click the **Table of Figures** tab.

» In the **Formats** list in the **General** frame, select the option that corresponds to the presentation you require for the table of figures. You can see the result in the **Print Preview** frame. To create a custom presentation, select the **From template** option and click the **Modify** button.

You can also see a Web Preview of the table of figures, which shows how it would appear in a Web browser.

» If you wish, indicate what elements should be included and how they are to be presented. Do you want to **Show page numbers**? If so, do you want to **Right align page numbers**?

» For all the **Formats**, except **Centered**, specify whether or not you want to add a **Tab leader** between the entry and the page number, using the corresponding drop-down list.

» In the **Caption label** list, select the option that corresponds to the type of caption that should be taken into account when the table of figures is created. For example, if all the caption labels in your document are **Figure** and you choose **Table** in the **Caption label** list, instead of seeing a table of figures, you will see an error text saying that no entries were found for the table. Furthermore, if your document contains different types of caption, for example, **Figure** and **Table**, only the captions that correspond to the option chosen in the **Caption label** list will appear in the table of figures.

※ Deactivate the **Include label and number** option if you do not want to include the caption labels (e.g. **Equation**, **Table** or **Figure**) in the table of figures. In this case the only caption labels visible in the table of figures will be those to which you have added custom text.

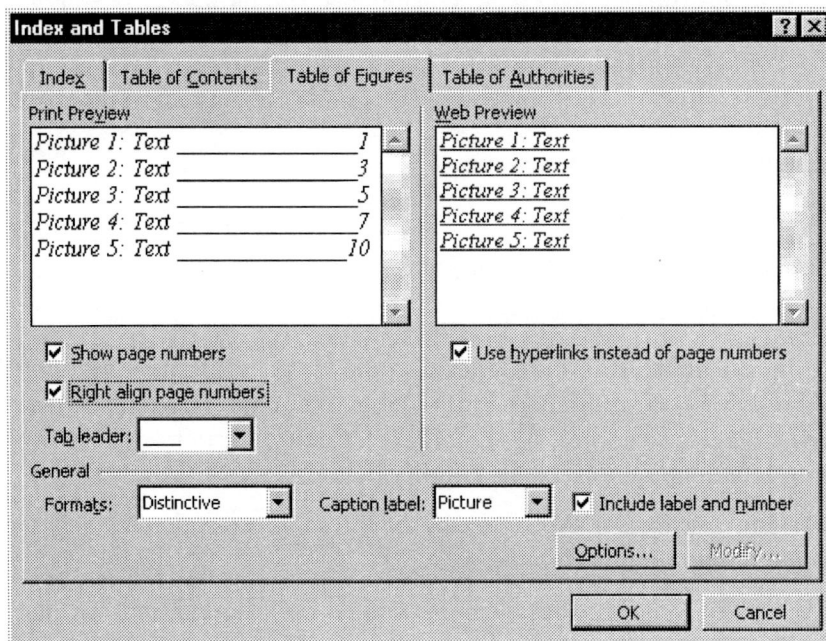

※ If you intend to display your table of figures in a Web browser and you want a hyperlink to be created for each heading, make sure the **Use hyperlinks instead of page numbers** option is active.

When this option is active, hyperlinks are created for each title in the table of figures inserted in the document, without removing the page numbers.

※ Click **OK**.

※ If required, use Alt F9 to hide the code corresponding to the table of figures and view the entries it contains.

*If the **Use hyperlinks instead of page numbers** option is active in the **Index and Tables** dialog box (**Table of Figures** tab), a hyperlink will be created for each entry in the table.*

* To go to a caption in the document, hold down the ⌷Ctrl⌷ key and click the corresponding title in the table of figures.

* To update a table of figures if you have added, deleted or modified any captions, click one of the entries in the table of figures and press the ⌷F9⌷ key. Choose to **Update page numbers only** or to **Update entire table** with the corresponding option then click **OK**.

📄 *When you select the table of figures, it appears with a grey background. You can choose to display this background permanently (or never at all) using the **Field shading** option in the **Options** dialog box (**Tools - Options - View** tab).*

*To change how the table of figures is presented, select another **Format** in the **Table of Figures** page of the **Index and Tables** dialog box (**Insert - Reference - Index and Tables**). Once you have confirmed your choice, the new presentation replaces the old one.*

9 ▪ Creating a table of authorities

A table of authorities is used for legal documents. It lists references to citations, concerning legal cases, statutes or laws.

Marking a citation

* Select the text of the long citation you want to mark.

* **Insert - Reference - Index and Tables**

* Click the **Table of Authorities** tab then click the **Mark Citation** button.

* If required, modify the citation text that appears in the **Selected text** box, so it appears as you want it to in the table of authorities.

* Select an option in the **Category** list that describes what your citation is.

▪ If you wish, format the text in the **Selected text** box. To do this, select the text concerned, right-click the selection, click the **Font** option then choose the type of formatting you want to apply. Click **OK**.

▪ If the active citation (selected text) appears in the document as a short citation and you also want to mark this, change the text in the **Short citation** box so it corresponds to the short citation that Microsoft Word has to find in the document.

▪ Click the **Mark** button to mark the active citation (just the one selected in the document) or the **Mark All** button to mark the active citation and all the long and short citations that correspond to those shown in the **Mark Citation** dialog box.

▪ To mark a new citation, click the **Next Citation** button once or several times until you reach the required citation in the document (the **Next Citation** button looks for words and abbreviations usually found in citations, such as article, statute etc). You can also click the **Close** button on the **Mark Citation** dialog box and select the text that corresponds to the next citation you wish to mark.

📄 *The **Category** button on the **Mark Citation** dialog box (**Insert - Reference - Index and tables - Mark Citation** button) can be used to rename the existing categories. To do this, select the name of the **Category** you wish to rename in the corresponding list box, type the new name in the **Replace with** text box and click the **Replace** button.*

Inserting a table of authorities

※ Place the insertion point where you want the table of authorities to appear.

※ **Insert - Reference - Index and Tables**

※ Click the **Table of Authorities** tab.

※ In the **Category** list box, select the name of the category you want to include in the table of authorities or select the **All** option to include all the categories. When you choose **All**, Word inserts a table for each category it finds in the document.

※ In the **Formats** list, select the option that corresponds to the presentation you require for the table of figures. You can see the result in the **Print Preview** frame. To create a custom presentation, select the **From template** option and click the **Modify** button.

※ Indicate whether you wish to add a **Tab leader** between the entries and the page numbers.

※ Deactivate the **Use passim** option if you do not want the term "Passim" to be used; this normally replaces references when there are more than five references on a page that refer to the same citation.

※ Deactivate the **Keep original formatting** option if you do not want to keep the character formats for long citations that were applied in the **Selected text** box in the **Mark Citation** dialog box when the citation was marked.

Index and Tables ? X

Index | Table of Contents | Table of Figures | **Table of Authorities**

Print Preview

Category:

CASES

Baldwin v. Alberti,
58 Wn. 2d 243 (1961)-------- 5, 6
Dravo Corp. v. Metro. Seattle,
79 Wn. 2d 214 (1971)-----passim
Forrester v. Craddock.

All
Cases
Statutes
Other Authorities
Rules
Treatises
Regulations
Constitutional Provisions
Local Acts

☑ Use passim

☑ Keep original formatting

Tab leader: -------

Formats: Formal

Mark Citation... | Modify...

OK | Cancel

* Click **OK**.

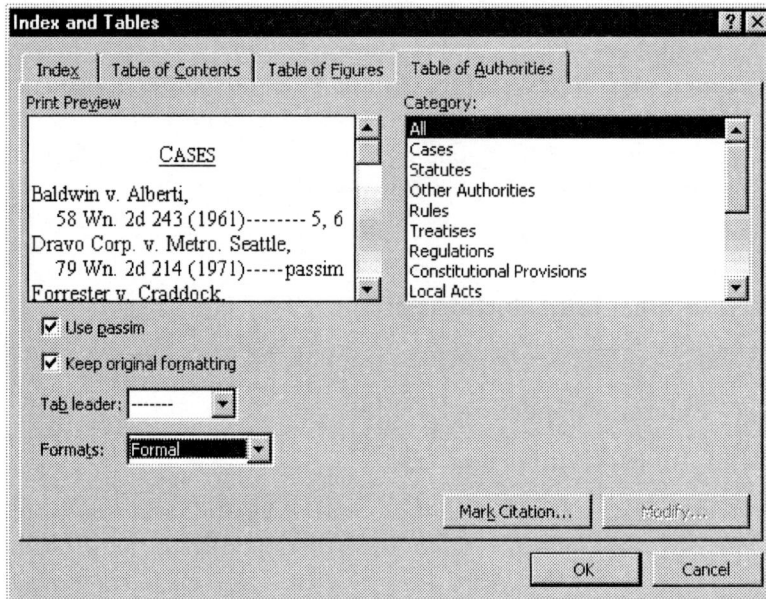

* If required, use `Alt` `F9` to hide the code corresponding to the table of contents and view the entries it contains.

* To update a table of authorities if you have added, deleted or modified any citations, click one of the entries in the table of authorities and press the `F9` key.

📄 *When you select the table of authorities, it appears with a grey background. You can choose to display this background permanently (or never at all) using the **Field shading** option in the **Options** dialog box (**Tools - Options - View** tab).*

*To change how the table of authorities is presented, select another format in the **Table of Authorities** page of the **Index and Tables** dialog box (**Insert - Reference - Index and Tables**). Once you have confirmed your choice, the new presentation replaces the old one.*

Below, you can see **Practice Exercise** 2.3. This exercise is made up of 9 steps. If you do not know how to do one of the steps, go back to the title that corresponds to that particular lesson. When you have finished, you can check your work by reading the **Solution** that follows.

Steps in the exercise that are likely to be tested on the exam are preceded by this symbol: 🏛. However, it is a good idea to complete all the steps in the exercise, to ensure that you have understood all the points discussed in the lesson.

👉 Practice Exercise 2.3

To work on practice exercise 2.3, open the **2-3 Getting around in Florida.doc** *document, located in the* **MOUS Word 2002 Expert** *folder.*

1. Display the document in **Outline** view and make an outline of the document, applying the following styles to the appropriate headings:

Heading	Style to apply
DRIVING	Heading 1
Traffic	Heading 2
Signs	Heading 2
If you break down	Heading 2
TRANSPORT	Heading1
By air	Heading 2
By road	Heading 2
Hire cars	Heading 3
Chauffeur-driven cars	Heading 3
Motorbikes	Heading 3
Coaches	Heading 3
By train	Heading 2

Return to **Print Layout** view.

2. Apply an outline **Level 4** to paragraphs with the **VL subheading** style (Conditions, Details, Hiring a car).

3. Go into **Outline** view and show all the headings of **Level 3** and above.

   Move the **By air** heading to after the **By train** heading, to achieve the following result:

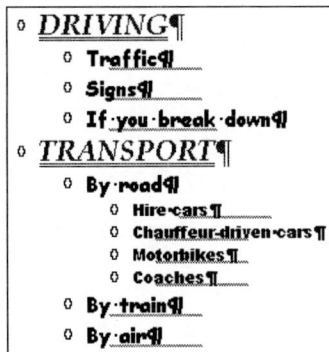

   Finish by printing the document outline (remember that the document outline contains four outline levels) then return to **Print Layout** view.

4. Insert a table of contents in the last paragraph of page 2. Use the **Formal** format and show headings up to level 4.

5. Apply a **Heading 2** style to the **American cars** title (page 4) and the **VL subheading** style to the style to the **Cost** and **Fuel** titles on page 6.
   Next, update the table of contents then close the **2-3 Getting around in Florida.doc** document, saving the changes made.

6. To continue exercise 2.3, open the **2-3 Getting around in Florida 2.doc** document in the **MOUS Word 2002 Expert** folder.

   To the right of the **Signs** heading (page 3), create the following index entry:
   Driving
       Signs

To the right of the **By road** heading (page 5), create the following index entry:

Transport
> **By road**

To the right of the **Motorbikes** heading (page 6), create the following index entry:

Motorbike
> **Hire**

For each of these index entries, the page number is to be shown in the index.

Other index entries have been created already in the document; insert the index table at the end of the document, using the same presentation as the extract shown below:

B		*M*	
Breakdown 4		Motorbike	
		Hire 6	
		Motoribike	
C		Travelling 6	
Car		*P*	
Chauffeur driven 6			
Cost 6		Petrol	
Fuel 6		Car 6	
Hire car conditions 5		Plane 7	
Hire car details 5			
How to hire a car 5			

7. To the right of the **Motorbikes** heading (page 6), insert this index entry:
Travelling
> **Motorbike**

Update the index table then close the **2-3 Getting around in Florida 2.doc** document, saving the changes made.

8. To continue exercise 2.3, open the **2-3 Travel Pictures.doc** in the **MOUS Word 2002 Expert**.

Give the caption **Picture 7 Winter sports** under the **last** picture on page **2**. Other captions have been inserted into the document already; insert the table of figures at the end of the document, using the same presentation as the extract shown below:

Picture 1 Space Shuttle	*1*
Picture 2 Sea Cruise	*1*
Picture 3 Luggage	*1*
Picture 4 Party Time!	*2*
Picture 5 Taking it easy	*2*
Picture 6 Egyptian Sunset	*2*
Picture 7 Winter sports	*2*
Picture 8 Airport	*3*
Picture 9 Taking the coach	*3*

Delete the **third** picture on page **1** as well as its caption then update the table of figures.

When you have finished, close the **2-3 Travel Pictures.doc** document, saving the changes made.

9. To continue exercise 2.3, open the **2-3 Fraud Act.doc** document in the **MOUS Word 2002 Expert** folder.

Rename categories **8**, **9** and **10** as follows:

rename category 8 as **Local Acts**,

rename category 9 as **Articles**,

rename category 10 as **By-Laws**.

As several citations have been entered already, insert the table of authorities at the end of the document, using the same presentation as in the extract below:

STATUTES

Banking Act 1987 (c. 22)--2
Banking Co-ordination (Second Council Directive) Regulations 1992 (S.I. 1992/3218) ------------------------------2
Contributions and Benefits Act--1
Electricity Act 1989--2

LOCAL ACTS

Jobseekers (Northern Ireland) Order 1995 (S.I. 1995/2705 (N.I. 15)---5
Local Government etc. (Scotland) Act 1994 --2
Local Government etc. (Scotland) Act 1994 (c. 39)--1

Finish by closing the **2-3 Fraud Act.doc** document, saving the changes made.

If you would like to practise these features more, on another document, you should work through Summary Exercise 2, on LONG DOCUMENTS. You will find the summary exercises at the end of the book.

It is often possible to perform a task in several different ways, but here, only the easiest solution is presented. You can go back to the corresponding lesson if you want to see other techniques you could use.

Solution to Exercise 2.3

1. To display the document in Outline view, use the **View - Outline** command.
   To apply the specified style to each of the headings as described in the table in step 1 of this exercise, perform the following actions:
   - click the heading mentioned (for example, DRIVING),
   - open the **Style** list on the **Formatting** toolbar,
   - click the name of the style you wish to apply (for example, Heading 1).

   To return to Print Layout view, use the **View - Print Layout** command.

2. To apply a "Level 4" outline level to the paragraphs with the "VL subheading" style, make sure the insertion point is not positioned in a paragraph with a preset heading style. Click the ⌷ tool button on the **Formatting** toolbar to display the **Styles and Formatting** task pane.
   In the **Pick formatting to apply** list, point to the **VL subheading** style, click the ⌷ button that appears and choose **Modify**.
   Click the **Format** button and then the **Paragraph** option.
   Open the **Outline level** list and click the **Level 4** option.
   Click **OK** twice.

3. To go into Outline view, use the **View - Outline** command. To see all the headings from Level 3 and above, open the `Show Level 4 ▾` list on the **Outlining** toolbar and click **Show Level 3**.

   To move the "By air" title underneath the "By train" title, point to the plus sign to the left of the **By air** text and drag it beneath the **By train** text.

To print the document outline, open the `Show Level 4 ▾` list on the **Outlining** toolbar, choose **Level 4** to display all the document headings and click the 🖶 tool button.

To return to Print Layout view, use the **View - Print Layout** command.

4. To insert the table of contents, click the last paragraph on page 2, activate the **Insert - Reference - Index and Tables** command and click the **Table of Contents** tab.
Open the **Formats** list then click the **Formal** choice.
Enter **4** in the **Show levels** box and click **OK**.

5. To apply a "Heading 2" style to the "American cars" heading, click this text, and in the **Style** list, click the **Heading 2** style.

To apply the "VL subheading" style to the "Cost" heading, click this text and in the **Style** list, click the **VL subheading** style.

To apply the "VL subheading" style to the "Fuel" heading, click this text and in the **Style** list, click the **VL subheading** style.

To update the table of contents, click one of the headings within it and press `F9`.
Activate the **Update entire table** option and click **OK**.

To close the 2-3 Getting around in Florida.doc document, saving the changes you have made, use the **File - Close** command and click **Yes** on the message that asks you if you would like to save the changes you have made.

6. To create an index entry next to the "Signs" heading, click at the end of the heading text and press `Alt` `Shift` **X**.
Type **Driving** in the **Main entry** box and **Signs** in the **Subentry** box then click **Mark** and finally **Close**.

To create an index entry next to the "By road" heading, click at the end of this heading, after the existing index entry, and press `Alt` `Shift` **X**.

Type **Transport** in the **Main entry** box and **By road** in the **Subentry** box, click **Mark** then **Close**.

To create an index entry next to the "Motorbikes" heading, click the end of the existing entries that follow the heading (page 6) and press ⌨Alt ⌨Shift **X**.
Type **Motorbike** in the **Main entry** box and **Hire** in the **Subentry** box, click **Mark** then **Close**.

To insert an index based on the presentation shown in step 6 of the exercise, first press ⌨Ctrl ⌨End to go to the end of the document.
Use the **Insert - Reference - Index and Tables** command and click the **Index** tab.
Open the **Formats** list and click the **Modern** choice.
Tick the **Right align page numbers** option, select the first style in the **Tab leader** list (dots) and click **OK**.

7. To create an index entry to the right of the "Motorbikes" heading, click the end of the heading and press ⌨Alt ⌨Shift **X**.
Type **Travelling** in the **Main entry** box and **Motorbike** in the **Subentry** box and click the **Mark** button then **Close**.

To update the index, click the table and press ⌨F9.

To close the 2-3 Getting around in Florida 2.doc document, saving the changes, use the **File - Close** command and click the **Yes** button on the message asking you if you want to save your changes.

8. To add the caption "Picture 7 Winter sports" under the last picture on page 2, click the picture to select it then use the **Insert - Reference - Caption** command.
Click the **New Label** button, type the text **Picture** in the **Caption** text box and click **OK**.
If necessary, click after the number **7** in the **Caption** text box, press the ⌨Space bar and enter the text **Winter sports**.
Make sure the **Below selected item** option is selected in the **Position** list then click **OK**.

To insert the table of figures at the end of the document, basing its presentation on the sample shown in step 8, press `Ctrl` `End` to go to the end of the document. Use the **Insert - Reference - Index and Tables** command then click the **Table of Figures** tab.
Open the **Formats** list and choose the **Distinctive** style.
If necessary, open the **Caption label** list and select the **Picture** option then click **OK**.

To delete the third picture on page 1 and its caption, drag in the left margin to select the picture and its caption then press the `Del` key.

To update the table of figures, click one of the entries in it and press `F9`.

To close and save the 2-3 Travel Pictures.doc document, use the **File - Close** command and click **Yes** on the message that asks if you want to save your changes.

9. To rename categories 8, 9 and 10, use the **Insert - Reference - Index and Tables** command then click the **Table of Authorities** tab.
Click the **Mark Citation** button then the **Category** button.
Click **8** in the **Category** list, select whatever is in the **Replace with** text box and type **Local Acts** then click the **Replace** button.
Click **9** in the **Category** list, select whatever is in the **Replace with** text box and type **Articles** then click the **Replace** button.
Click **10** in the **Category** list, select whatever is in the **Replace with** text box and type **By-Laws** then click the **Replace** button.
Click **OK** then **Close**.

To insert, at the end of the document, the tables of authorities for all the categories present in the document, based on the examples shown in step 9, press `Ctrl` `End` to go to the end of the document. Use the **Insert - Reference - Index and Tables** command then click the **Table of Authorities** tab.
Select the **All** option in the **Category** list.
Open the **Formats** list then click the **Formal** choice.
Click **OK**.

To close and save the 2-3 Fraud Act.doc document, use the **File - Close** command and click **Yes** on the message that asks if you want to save your changes.

LONG DOCUMENTS
Lesson 2.4: Master documents

▥1 ▪ **Creating a master document**

A master document brings together a group of associated documents called sub-documents. A long document can sometimes be managed more easily by splitting it into several sub-documents.

▪ Create a new document using the template common to all the sub-documents.

▪ **View - Outline**

*Word displays the **Outlining** toolbar (this can be moved if you cannot see all its tools).*

▪ If necessary, click the ▢ tool button to activate the **Master Document View** and display the corresponding tools.

▪ To insert a sub-document, click the ▦ tool button, select the document you wish to insert and click the **Open** button.

The whole sub-document appears surrounded by a grey border.

▪ To show only the outline of the sub-document, open the [Show Level 4 ▾] list on the **Outlining** toolbar then click the required level depending on which headings you wish to see.

▪ Save the master document then close it.

▥2 ▪ **Using a master document**

▪ Open the master document that contains the sub-documents.

When you open a master document, it is condensed, with each sub-document appearing as a hyperlink. You can [Ctrl]-click the hyperlink to open the sub-document. When the non-printing characters are on display, you can see that sub-documents are separated by section breaks.

▪ Click the ▦ tool button to expand the sub-documents.

» Choose what you wish to see using the tools on the **Outlining** toolbar.

» To open a sub-document, double-click the sub-document icon (▤) that appears in the top left corner of the frame. When you have finished working on it, close the sub-document before coming back to the master document.

If you do not close it, the sub-document will be locked in the master document (you will see a padlock symbol appear above the ▤ icon) and you will not be able to make any changes to it.

» To lock a sub-document to prevent any changes being made, click in the sub-document concerned then click the ⊞ tool button. To unlock, click the ⊞ tool button again.

» To reorganise the contents of the master document, select within the sub-document the heading(s) you wish to move then use the ⬆ or ⬇ tool button. Alternatively, point to the cross preceding the heading and drag it to its new position.

To move items, you can also drag them with the mouse or use the ✄ and ▤ tools.

» To divide a sub-document, position the insertion point at the place where you wish to break up the sub-document and click ▤.

The ▤ tool button is only available if the insertion point is located at the beginning of a paragraph.

» To merge sub-documents, select them then click the ▤ tool button; to select sub-documents, select the first sub-document you wish to merge by clicking its ▤ icon, hold down the ⟨Shift⟩ key then click the last ▤ icon in the group of sub-documents you require.

The ▤ tool button will only be available if no paragraph (not even a blank paragraph) is selected outside the frames of the sub-documents being merged.

* To delete a sub-document, select the sub-document by clicking its 🗒 icon then press the ⬚Del⬚ key.

  When this is done, the sub-document will no longer be part of the master document. You can however continue to use it as a normal Word document.

* To insert or delete page or section breaks in a master document, you should show the non-printing characters then proceed as you would for a document in **Normal** or **Print Layout** view.

* If you wish to number the headings or pages, or insert a table of contents or an index or create headers and footers and so on, proceed as you would on any other document.

* To print all the sub-documents, print the master document.

Below, you can see **Practice Exercise** 2.4. This exercise is made up of 2 steps. If you do not know how to do one of the steps, go back to the title that corresponds to that particular lesson. When you have finished, you can check your work by reading the **Solution** that follows.

All the parts of this exercise are likely to be tested on the MOUS exam.

☞ Practice Exercise 2.4

1. Create a master document and insert, in this order, the sub-documents **2-4 Florida Daily Life.doc** then **2-4 Driving in Florida.doc**, which are in the **MOUS Word 2002 Expert** folder.

   Save the master document as **2-4 FLORIDA.doc**, placing it in the **MOUS Word 2002 Expert** folder, then close it.

2. Open the **2-4 FLORIDA.doc** master document and make the following changes to it:

   - delete the last paragraph marker (¶) in the master document.

   - expand the sub-documents to see their contents.

   - delete the **Section Break (Next Page)** at the top of the document.

   - show all headings of level 4 and above.

   - move the **Drinks** heading to after the heading **Ethnic cuisine in Florida**.

   - split the second sub-document at the **TRANSPORT** heading.

   - open the last sub-document to delete the picture on page 1 then close it, saving it in the **MOUS Word 2002 Expert** folder under the name **3-3 Getting around in Florida.doc**

   - number the headings in the outline as shown below (a preset style has been applied to each heading).

```
◊ I.  FOOD
     ◊ A. Meals
     ◊ B. Florida specialities
     ◊ C. Ethnic cuisine in Florida
     ◊ D. Drinks
◊ II. FESTIVALS AND HOLIDAYS
     ◊ A. Festivals and carnivals
     ◊ B. National holidays
◊ III. TO SMOKE OR NOT TO SMOKE
◊ IV.    TIPS
◊ V. DISABLED CITIZENS
◊ VI.    OPENING HOURS
◊ VII.   COURTESY
◊ VIII.  SAFETY
```

- save the changes made to the master document.

- show the master document in print preview then print it.

- close the master document.

If you would like to practise these features more, on another document, you should work through Summary Exercise 2, on LONG DOCUMENTS. You will find the summary exercises at the end of the book.

It is often possible to perform a task in several different ways, but here, only the easiest solution is presented. You can go back to the corresponding lesson if you want to see other techniques you could use.

Solution to Exercise 2.4

1. To create a master document, click the ☐ tool button to create a new document then use the **View - Outline** command.

   If necessary, activate the ▦ tool button on the **Outlining** toolbar to activate the **Master Document View**.

   To insert the first sub-document, click the 🗗 tool button, select the **MOUS Word 2002 Expert** folder and double-click the **2-4 Florida Daily Life.doc**.

   To insert the second sub-document, click the 🗗 tool button then double-click the **2-4 Driving in Florida.doc** document in the **MOUS Word 2002 Expert** folder.

   To save the master document, click the 🖫 tool button, select the **MOUS Word 2002 Expert** folder, type **2-4 FLORIDA.doc** in the **File name** text box and click the **Save** button.
   To close the master document, use the **File - Close** command.

2. To open the 2-4 FLORIDA.doc, click the 🖃 tool button, select the **MOUS Word 2002 Expert** folder then double-click the **2-4 FLORIDA.doc** file.

   If they are not visible, show the non-printing characters by clicking the ¶ tool button.

   To delete the last paragraph marker in the master document, click the marker and press the Del key.

To expand the sub-documents, click the [icon] tool button on the **Outlining** toolbar.

To delete the **Section Break (Next Page)** at the top of the document, click the break and press the [Del] key.

To show all headings of level 4 and above, open the **Show Level** list [Show Level 4 ▾] on the **Outlining** toolbar and click the **Show Level 4** option.

To move the "Drinks" heading underneath the "Ethnic cuisine in Florida" heading, point to the plus sign that precedes **Drinks** and drag the heading under the **Ethnic cuisine in Florida** heading.

To split the second sub-document at the **TRANSPORT** heading, place the insertion point before the **T** in the **TRANSPORT** heading and click the [icon] tool button on the **Outlining** toolbar.

To open the last sub-document and delete the picture, double-click the sub-document icon [icon], click the picture you can see on page 1 then press the [Del] key.

To close and save the sub-document, use the **File - Close** command and click **Yes** on the message that asks if you want to save your changes. Next, type **2-4 Getting around in Florida.doc** in the **File name** text box, select the **MOUS Word 2002 Expert** folder if necessary then click the **Save** button.

To number the headings in the outline as shown in step 2, place the insertion point in any sub-document, use the **Format - Bullets and Numbering** command then click the **Outline Numbered** tab. Select the third choice on the second row and click **OK**.

To save the changes made to the master document, click the [icon] tool button.

To show the master document in the print preview, click the [icon] tool button then click [icon] to print it.

To close the master document, use the **File - Close** command.

MAIL MERGE
Lesson 3.1: Forms

1 ▪ Creating a form

A form is a document that contains some permanent text and spaces for filling in variable data. Here is an example:

YOUR DETAILS

Title: ▢   Surname: ▢   First name: ▢

Address: ▢

City: ▢   Postcode: ▢

☎ home: ▢   From: ▢ to ▢ (hours)

☎ work: ▢   From: ▢ to ▢ (hours)

FLIGHT

Flight		Number of passengers		
Return ▢ One-way ▢		Adults	Children	Infants
ALL AIRLINES		▢	▢ *(-12)*	▢ *(-2)*

▪ Create or modify a document template.

▪ Enter the permanent text.

▪ At each place you wish to enter variable data, insert a form field using the **Forms** toolbar (cf. below).

▪ When you have completed the form, protect it (cf. Protecting a form) and save it.

▥2 ▪ Inserting form fields

A form field can be presented as a text box, a drop-down list or a check box.

▪ Show the **Forms** toolbar with the **View - Toolbars - Forms** command.

▪ Position the insertion point where the field should appear.

▪ Click the ⌷ab⌷ tool button to insert a **Text** field, the ⌷☑⌷ tool button to insert a **Check Box** field or the ⌷▦⌷ tool button to insert a **Drop-down** field.

A greyed-out form field appears in the document.

▪ Define the options that correspond to the field type you chose (cf. below).

> 📄 *If field codes are displayed (⌷Alt⌷⌷F9⌷), the form fields appear as follows: {FORMTEXT} for a text field, {FORMCHECKBOX} for a check box field and {FORMDROPDOWN} for a drop-down list field.*
>
> *These three form fields can only be used if the document is protected as a form.*

▥3 ▪ Defining text field properties

▪ Click the **Text** field concerned then click the ⌷▦⌷ tool button on the **Forms** toolbar.

▪ Define what **Type** of text field it is.

▪ If required, set a **Default text** and a **Maximum length** for the field as well as its **Text format**.

Text Form Field Options [?] [X]

Text form field

Type:
Regular text ▼

Default text:

Maximum length:
Unlimited ▲▼

Text format:
Uppercase ▼

Run macro on

Entry:
▼

Exit:
▼

Field settings

Bookmark:
Text27

☑ Fill-in enabled

☐ Calculate on exit

Add Help Text... | OK | Cancel

* If you want a brief message to appear on the status bar, click the **Add Help Text** button and enter the text in the **Type your own** text box and click **OK**.

* Click **OK**.

4 ▪ Defining drop-down list field properties

* Click the drop-down list concerned then click the [tool icon] tool button.

* For each item you want to include in the list, enter it in the **Drop-down item** text box and click **Add**.

* If you want to remove an item, select it in the **Items in drop-down list** list and click **Remove**.

* If required, reorganise the list using the **Move** buttons.

* Click **Add Help Text** if you want to write a message that will appear when the insertion point is in the field.

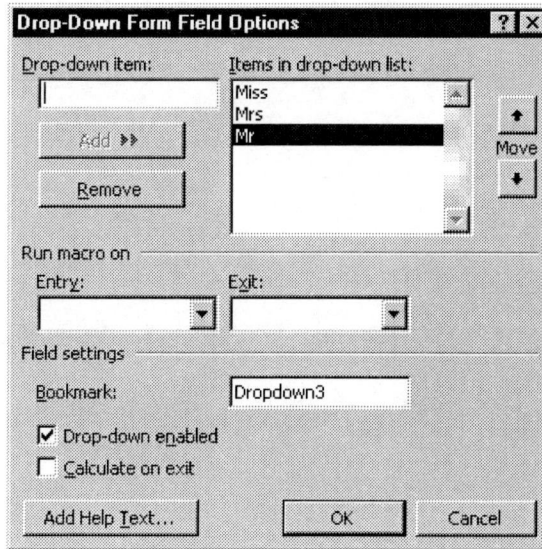

Drop-Down Form Field Options

Drop-down item:

Items in drop-down list:
- Miss
- Mrs
- **Mr**

Add ▶▶

Remove

Move ↑ ↓

Run macro on

Entry:

Exit:

Field settings

Bookmark: Dropdown3

☑ Drop-down enabled

☐ Calculate on exit

Add Help Text...   OK   Cancel

* Click **OK**.

The first name in the list is always suggested as the default field value.

5 ▪ Defining check box field properties

* Click the check box concerned then click ▣.

* Specify how you want the check box to look using the properties in the **Check box size** and **Default value** frames.

* If you wish, click **Add Help Text** and write your help message.

* Click **OK**.

🖫6 ▪ **Protecting a form**

* Make sure that the document is completely finished.

* **Tools - Protect Document**

* Activate the **Forms** option.

* If you wish, enter a **Password** with a maximum of 15 characters.

On the screen, asterisks (*) always replace the characters of the password. Be careful about the case of the letters you use.

▪ Click **OK**.

To be sure there are no mistakes, you must enter the password again.

▪ Enter the password a second time and click **OK**.

▪ Save the form and close it.

📄 *To remove the protection, use **Tools - Unprotect Document** and enter the password used to protect the document (if there is one) then click **OK**. Remember to take care with the case of characters.*

🔖 *The* 🔒 *tool button allows you to protect/unprotect a form without setting a password.*

7 ▪ Using a form

▪ Create a new document based on a form template.

The first form field is selected and its help text is displayed on the status bar. Because the document is protected as a form, access is authorised to the form fields only.

▪ Move from field to field using ⇥ and ⇧⇥ and fill in the fields with the required data.

Below, you can see **Practice Exercise** 3.1. This exercise is made up of 7 steps. If you do not know how to do one of the steps, go back to the title that corresponds to that particular lesson. When you have finished, you can check your work by reading the **Solution** that follows.

All the parts of this exercise are likely to be tested on the MOUS exam.

☞ **Practice Exercise 3.1**

To work on practice exercise 3.1, you will need to open the *3-1 Information sheet.dot* template in the *MOUS Templates* folder. Depending on your version of Windows, the default file path for the *Templates* folder could be *C:\Windows \Application Data\Microsoft\Templates* (for 98 and ME) or *C:\Documents and settings\user_name\Application Data\Microsoft\Templates* (for Windows 2000 Professional).

⊞ 1. Modify the document template by adding text as shown below:

If you can see the field codes, hide them.

2. In the form, insert text form fields after the tab stops that follows the **Surname** and **First Name** labels, a drop-down list field after the tab stop that follows **Title** and a check box field after the tab stop that follows **One-way** (in the first table). If you cannot see the non-printing characters, you may want to display them to make it easier to insert these fields (you can hide them again later, if you wish). You should obtain the result below:

YOUR DETAILS

Title: ▓   Surname: ▓   First name: ▓

Address: ▓

City: ▓   Postcode: ▓

☎ home: ▓   From: ▓ to ▓ (hours)

☎ work: ▓   From: ▓ to ▓ (hours)

FLIGHT

Flight		Number of passengers		
Return ☐ One-way ☐		Adults	Children	Infants
ALL AIRLINES		▓	▓ (-12)	▓ (-2)

3. Define the properties of the text form fields that follow **Surname** and **Postcode** as follows:

Surname   Regular text, unlimited maximum length, UPPERCASE formatting.

Postcode   Regular text, maximum length **7** characters.

4. Define the properties of the drop-down form field to the right of the **Title** label, so the list contains the options **Miss**, **Mrs** and **Mr**.

5. Define the properties of the check box form field to the right of **Return** so that the check box is active by default.

🔲 6. Protect the form, using the password **form** (in lowercase letters). Save the changes made to the form and close it.

🔲 7. Use the **3-1 Information sheet.dot** template to fill out the form fields as shown below:

FLOR TOUR

Date: 4 September 2001

Planning your next holiday?
Fill out this form to help us offer you a better service.

YOUR DETAILS

Title: Mrs   Surname: **WARD**   First name: Christine

Address: 14 Bailey Rd

City: Paisley   Postcode: PA1 2BS

☎ home: 0141 555 4400   From: 18:00   to   22:00   (hours)

☎ work: 0141 555 2233   From: 8:30   to   17:00   (hours)

FLIGHT

Flight		Number of passengers		
Return ☒ One-way ☐		Adults 2	Children (-12)	Infants (-2)

Route	Depart	Arrive	Departure date
Outbound	Glasgow	Miami	05/10/01
Return	Miami	Glasgow	20/10/01

ACCOMMODATION

Number of rooms				
Single	Double	Triple	Family	Category
		1		2**

Location	Arrival date	Number of nights
Miami	06/10/2001	14

If you would like to practise these features more, on another document, you should work through Summary Exercise 3, on MAIL MERGE. You will find the summary exercises at the end of the book.

It is often possible to perform a task in several different ways, but here, only the easiest solution is presented. You can go back to the corresponding lesson if you want to see other techniques you could use.

Solution to Exercise 3.1

1. To modify the document template, click the second paragraph after the text "Date" and type **Planning your next holiday?** and press ⏎. Next, type **Fill out this form to help us offer you a better service**. If you need to hide the field codes, press `Alt` `F9`.

2. Before inserting the text form fields after "Surname" and "First name", click the ¶ tool button to display the non-printing characters then use the **View - Toolbars - Forms** command. Place the insertion point after the tab stop (→) that follows the text **Surname** then click `abl`. Next, place the insertion point after the tab stop (→) that follows **First name** and click `abl`. To insert a drop-down list after "Title", place the insertion point after the tab stop (→) that follows the **Title** label and click the 🖼 tool button. To insert a check box field after the "One-way" label, place the insertion point after the tab stop following the **One-way** label and click the ☑ tool button.

   To hide the non-printing characters, if necessary, click the ¶ tool button to deactivate it.

3. To set the properties of the text form field that follows the "Surname" label, click this field then click the 🖼 button on the **Forms** toolbar. Open the **Text format** list, click **Uppercase** and click **OK**. To set the properties for the text field that follows the "Postcode" label, click this field then click the 🖼 button on the **Forms** toolbar. Type **7** in the **Maximum length** box, and click **OK**.

181

4. To define the properties for the drop-down list on the "Title" field, click the field and then the ▣ tool button.
Enter **Miss** in the **Drop-down item** box then click **Add**. Enter **Mrs** in the **Drop-down item** box then click **Add**. Enter **Mr** in the **Drop-down item** box then click **Add**.
Finish by clicking **OK**.

5. To define the properties of the check box form field to the right of "Return", click the check box and click the ▣ tool button.
Activate the **Checked** option in the option in the **Default value** frame and click **OK**.

6. To protect the form, activate the **Tools - Protect Document** command and choose the **Forms** option.
Enter **form** (in lowercase letters) in the **Password** box and click **OK**. Enter the word **form** again (make sure it is in lowercase) and click **OK**. Save the changes made to the form by clicking the 🖫 tool button then close the form with **File - Close**.

7. To use the 3-1 Information sheet.dot template, use the **File - New** command then click the **General Templates** link in the **New Document** task pane. Click the **MOUS Templates** tab and double-click the **3-1 Information sheet** template.
Move from field to field using the ⭾ and ⇧⭾ keys and fill in the fields as shown in step 7.
If you like, save the document.

MAIL MERGE
Lesson 3.2: Mail merge

Step by step creation of a mail merge

*Word's **mail merge** function (also called a mailshot or mailout) can produce a number of copies of a document and link them to names, addresses or references contained in a separate data file.*

- Creating a mail merge requires at least two files:

  - a **main document**, containing the permanent text and the fields which will act as links to the data source file,

  - a **data file** containing the variable information.

- If it does not already exist, create the data source file: this should be made up of **fields** and **records**. For example:

First Name	Last Name	Address	City	Postcode
Fiona	Blackburn	15 Oak Drive	Salisbury	SAL 23X
Ross	Campbell	4A The Crescent	Winchester	WIN 11A

Each line of information, concerning for example Fiona Blackburn or Ross Campbell, is a record.

Each record is numbered according to the order in which it was entered or according to a sort order.

- If it does not already exist, create the main document.

- Link the data file to the main document.

- Insert the fields from the data file at the appropriate places in the main document.

- Start the mail merge.

⬛1 ▪ Creating a mail merge

To create a mail merge, you need to follow all the steps in the Mail Merge Wizard.

▪ You can use an existing document or template for your main document or you can create a new blank document with the **File - New** command and enter the permanent text.

▪ **Tools - Letters and Mailings - Mail Merge Wizard**

*The **Mail Merge** task pane appears on the screen:*

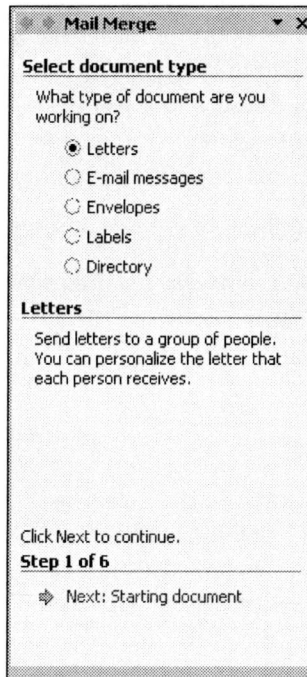

▪ Activate the **Letters** option in the **Select document type** section.

▪ Click the **Next: Starting document** link at the bottom of the task pane.

■ In the **Select starting document** section, select the option that describes what you wish to use as your main document:

Use the current document	The mail merge's main document is the active document.
Start from a template	The mail merge's main document is a ready to use mail merge template that you can customise if you wish. To choose a template, click the **Select template** link that appears in the **Start from a template** frame then double-click the name of the template you wish to use.
Start from existing document	The main document is based on an existing document. This could be an ordinary document or a main document used in a previous mail merge. If this can be seen in the **Start from existing** list box, select its name then click the **Open** button. Otherwise select the **(More files…)** option, click the **Open** button and select the required document. A new document based on the existing mail merge document appears on the screen.

■ Click the **Next: Select recipients** link to go to the next step.

*The **Previous: Select document type** link takes you back to the last step.*

■ Activate one of the options in the **Select recipients** section to select the list of addressees:

Use an existing list	You can select a file or database containing the list of recipients. To do this, click the **Browse** link under **Use an existing list** and select the file or database that contains the list of contacts. If required, modify the contents of the list then click **OK**. If the selected list is not what you were looking for, click the **Select a different list** link. *If your selected list of data is an Excel workbook (.xls) or an Access database, Word opens a dialog box when it opens the file so you can choose which worksheet in the workbook or which table in the database you want to use for the mailout.*

Select from Outlook contacts	You can select the list of recipients from your Outlook contacts folder. Click the **Choose Contacts folder** link in the **Select from Outlook contacts** section then double-click the name of the contacts folder that contains the required information. Modify the list of contacts if necessary then click **OK**.
Type a new list	Enter the contents of a new recipients list (cf. Creating a list of data, in this chapter).

▪ Click the **Next: Write your letter** link to go to the next step.

▪ Enter or modify as necessary the contents of the main document (the part of the text that remains the same).

▪ Insert the fields (the information referring to each recipient) into the main document. For each field you are inserting, follow this procedure:

- Place the insertion point where the field's contents should print.

- Click the **More items** link on the task pane, select the required field then click the **Insert** button and **Close**.

*The **Address block** link takes you to the **Insert Address Block** dialog box, which contains options for inserting recipient addresses in various forms [Address Block field]. The **Greeting line** link opens a dialog box, which you can use to insert greeting phrases to start your letter [Greeting Line].*

▪ Click the **Next: Preview your letters** link to go to the next step.

In the main document you can see a preview of the letter containing the information from the first record in the data list.

* Use the `<<` and `>>` buttons in the **Preview your letters** section to see a preview of the letter containing the information from the previous or next record.

  To **Find a recipient** in the list of data, click this link (cf. Managing the records in a data list, in this chapter).

* To exclude the active record from the mail merge, click the **Exclude this recipient** button in the **Make changes** frame.

* Click the **Next: Complete the merge** link to go to the next step.

* Click the **Print** link to merge to the printer and print the mailout letters or click the **Edit individual letters** link to create the merged letters in a new document.

- Specify which records should be merged. To merge all the records selected in the list of data, activate the **All** option. To merge the active record, click **Current record** (you cannot merge the current record if the records have been filtered). To merge using a group of records selected in the list of data, enter the number of the first record in the **From** text box then the last record in the **To** box.

- If you merge to a new document, make the required changes, print and/or save the document and close it.

- Save the main document and close it.

  If changes have been made to the list of data, Word prompts you to save them.

- If you wish, click **Yes** to save any changes made to the data list.

  *The **Edit recipients list** link that appears in steps 3 and 5 of the Mail Merge Wizard opens the **Mail Merge Recipients** dialog box so you can modify the contents of the data list (add, delete or edit records or filter them) or their presentation (sorting them).*

  *You can also insert a field into the main document by clicking the **Insert Merge Fields** tool button on the **Mail Merge** toolbar (**Tools - Letters and Mailings - Show Mail Merge Toolbar**).*

  *To run the mail merge, you can use the **Merge to New Document** and **Merge to Printer** tool buttons on the **Mail Merge** toolbar.*

2 ▪ Creating a list of data

- If the main document already exists, open it, otherwise create a new document in which you enter the fixed text for the mailshot.

- **Tools - Letters and Mailings - Mail Merge Wizard**

⁕ Click the **Next** link at the bottom of the task pane twice, until you reach step **3** of the Mail Merge Wizard.

⁕ Activate the **Type a new list** option in the **Select recipients** section and click the **Create** link.

*The **New Address List** dialog box appears on the screen, displaying a list of predefined fields.*

New Address List	? X

Enter Address information

Title	
First Name	
Last Name	
Company Name	
Address Line 1	
Address Line 2	
City	
State	

New Entry	Delete Entry	Find Entry ...	Filter and Sort...	Customize...

View Entries

View Entry Number	First	Previous	1	Next	Last

Total entries in list   1

Cancel

⁕ Click the **Customize** button to define the fields in the new list then follow these instructions:

- To delete a field, select it in the list, click the **Delete** button and click **Yes** to confirm the deletion.

- To add a new custom field, click the **Add** button, **Type a name for your field** in the corresponding text box and click **OK**.

   The customised field is added under the selected field.

- To rename a field, select it in the list, click the **Rename** button, enter the new name in the text box and click **OK**.

- To move a field, select it in the list then click the **Move Up** or **Move Down** button.

   Ideally, the fields should appear in the order in which you will be entering the data.

⊗ When the structure of the data file is satisfactory, click **OK**.

The data entry grid, containing the previously defined fields, reappears on the screen.

⊗ Click the text box of the first field.

⊗ For each record:

- Enter the data, using 🔲 to go to the next text box or 🔲 to return to the previous text box.

- After you have filled in the last field, press ⏎ twice or click the **New Entry** button to create a new record.

⊗ When you have finished entering all the records, click the **Close** button.

*The **Save Address List** dialog box appears on the screen.*

⊗ Enter a **File name** for the list of data and, if necessary, choose the folder in which to save it and click the **Save** button.

*The **Mail Merge Recipients** dialog box appears on the screen and shows you the list of data.*

Mail Merge Recipients

To sort the list, click the appropriate column heading. To narrow down the recipients displayed by a specific criteria, such as by city, click the arrow next to the column heading. Use the check boxes or buttons to add or remove recipients from the mail merge.

List of recipients:

	Last Name	First Name	Title	Address	City	Postcode
☑	Morrow	John	Mr	15 Crabtree ...	Ipswich	IPS 450
☑	Parker	Susan	Miss	2A Redland ...	Marlow	MAR 550
☑	Baverstock	Tania	Mrs	67 Milton Park	Dalby	DAL 990
☑	Davis	Virginia	Miss	5 Freers Drive	Marlow	MAR 440
☑	Chambers	Ross	Mr	88 Bluebell St	Blackt...	BLA 440
☑	Tully	Maureen	Miss	454 Marine ...	North ...	NOR 660
☑	Holt	Duncan	Mr	9 Hurst St	Roma ...	ROM 220
☑	Sutcliffe	Anne	Mrs	69B Farley Rd	Nellingt...	NEL 440
☑	Pearce	Lea	Miss	11 Forman St	Abbyville	ABB 330
☑						

Select All   Clear All   Refresh

Find...   Edit...   Validate   OK

* Click **OK**.

*You return to the main document. The **Mail Merge** toolbar may appear on the screen. This contains tools relevant to the mail merge feature.*

3 ▪ Managing the records in a data list

You can only use the data entry grid to manage a data list created during the mail merge setup or an existing list in a Word document (.doc). If you are using a list contained in an Excel worksheet (.xls) or a table in an Access database (.mdb), you will have to work on the list of records by opening the relevant file in its own application.

Going to the data entry grid

* Open the main document.

* If necessary, display the **Mail Merge** toolbar, using the **View - Toolbars - Mail Merge** command or with **Tools - Letters and Mailings - Show Mail Merge Toolbar**.

- Click the **Mail Merge Recipients** tool button ▣ on the **Mail Merge** toolbar.
- Click the **Edit** button.

  The grid opens and you can see the first record.

  The look and titles of the buttons in the entry grid dialog box differ depending on the file type of the data list (which may be a Word file (*.doc) or a Microsoft Office Address List (*.mdb).

- Use the buttons in the **View Entries** frame at the bottom of the entry grid to scroll through the records.

Adding a record

- Go to the data entry grid.
- Click the **Add New** or **New Entry** button (whichever is shown).

  *A blank grid appears and the current **Entry Number** changes.*

- Type the data for the new record and when you have entered the last field, press ⏎ to enter another new record or click **Close** to close the entry grid.

  The new records are added to the end of the list.

- Click **OK** on the **Mail Merge Recipients** dialog box.

Finding a record

- Go to the entry grid.
- Go to the first record by clicking the ⏮ button or the **First** button, whichever appears.
- Click either **Find** or **Find Entry**.
- In the **Find** or **Find What** box, enter the value you are looking for.
- In the **In field** or **This field** box (whichever appears), select the name of the field containing the value.

> **Find Entry** ? ✕
>
> Find: Holt
>
> Look in: ○ All fields
>   ● This field: Last Name   ▼
>
>   Find Next   Cancel

*The **All fields** option is only available when the list of data was entered during the mail merge process and carries out the search in all the fields in the list.*

* Start the search by clicking **Find First** or **Find Next** then click **Find Next** as many times as necessary until you reach the required record.

* Click the **Close** button when you have finished searching. A **Cancel** button may appear instead of **Close**; in this case, click **Cancel**.

* Click **Close** (or **Cancel**) to close the entry grid.

* Click **OK** on the **Mail Merge Recipients** dialog box.

*You can also look for a record by clicking the **Find Entry** tool button 🔍 on the **Mail Merge** toolbar.*

Deleting a record

* Go to the entry grid.

* Go to the record you wish to delete.

* Click the **Delete** or **Delete Entry** button.

* If necessary, click the **Yes** button to confirm the deletion.

* Click the **Close** button then click **OK**.

Editing a record

» Go to the entry grid.

» Go to the record you wish to modify.

» Make your changes.

» If you notice a mistake, click the **Restore** button (if it is available) to retrieve the original data.

» Click **Close** then **OK**.

> *To modify the structure of a data list, open the corresponding data file as a document (the records appear in a table). Make your changes as required and save the document.*

4 ▪ Setting criteria on a mail merge

Filtering by one value on one or more fields

Each field is in fact a list that you can open by clicking the arrowhead that appears at the right of the field name.

» Open the main document and if it is not on the screen, display the **Mail Merge** toolbar.

» Click the  tool button on the **Mail Merge** toolbar.

» For each field you wish to filter:

- Open the list on the field concerned.

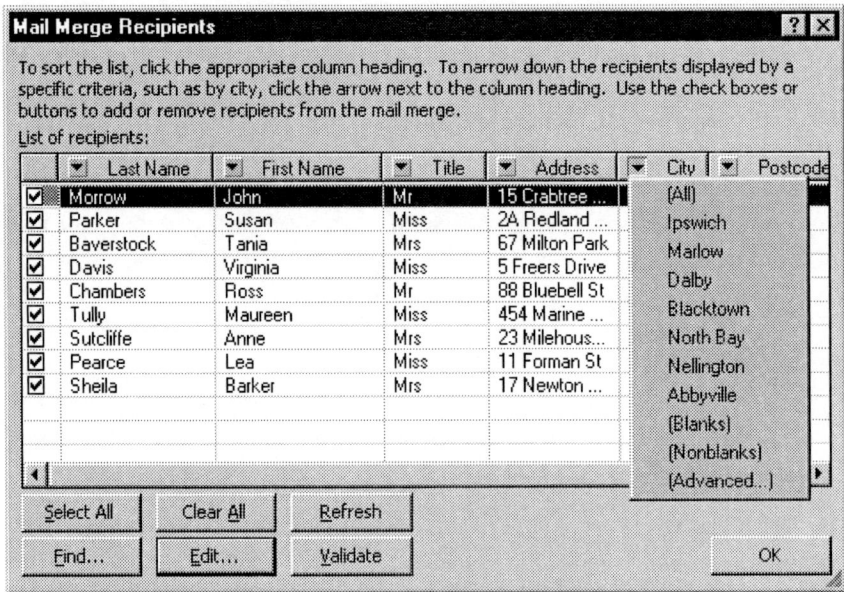

Each list contains all the values in that field and the **(All)**, **(Blanks)**, **(Nonblanks)** and **(Advanced)** options.

- Click the value you require. The **(Blanks)** option show all the record who do not have a value in that field and inversely the **(Nonblanks)** option shows all the records that do have a value in the field.

Only the records that meet your filter criterion are displayed. The arrow on the field names appears in blue when that field is filtered.

■ To remove the filter from a field and show all its records again, open the field list and choose the **(All)** option.

A checkbox appears to the left of each recipient's name in the **Mail Merge Recipients** dialog box (which you open by clicking). Tick the box to select or remove the tick to deselect that record for the mail merge. The **Select All** button will select all records once again and the **Clear All** button will deselect all the records.

Filtering on several values from one or more fields

❋ Open the main document and if it is not on the screen, display the **Mail Merge** toolbar.

❋ Click the ▨ tool button on the **Mail Merge** toolbar.

❋ Open the list associated with one of the fields then click the **(Advanced)** option.

❋ If necessary, click the **Filter Records** tab.

❋ For each criterion you wish to set:

- Select the name of the field in the **Field** list.

    The (none) option can be used to clear that particular criteria row.

- If necessary, modify the **Comparison** operator using the corresponding list.

- Click the **Compare to** box and enter the value you require.

- If you do want to set any other criteria, click **OK**.

- To set other criteria, choose the linking operator: select **And** to test the two conditions simultaneously or **Or** if one or the other condition can be met. Give the criteria.

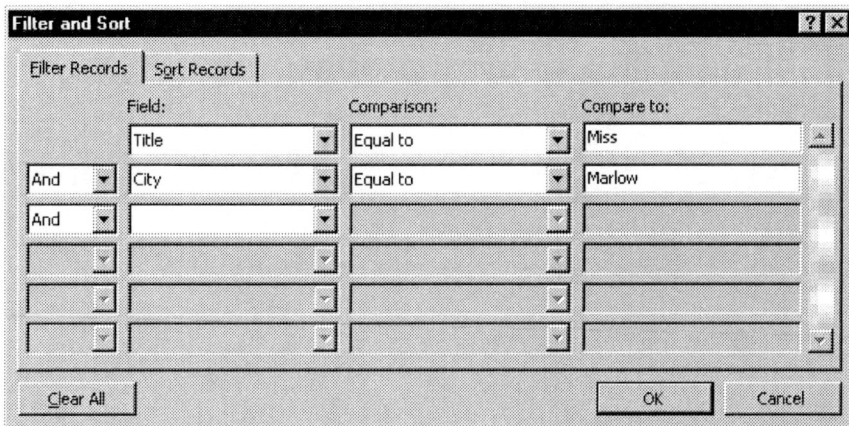

❋ Click **OK**.

*The filtered list appears in the **Mail Merge Recipients** dialog box.*

▪ Click **OK**.

The set criteria are saved within the main document.

*To delete all set criteria, click the **Clear All** button on the **Query Options** or **Filter and Sort** dialog box (this depends on whether or not the address list is a Word document (.doc)).*

5 ▪ Setting conditions for printing a text

You can set a condition so this text or that text will be displayed depending on the outcome.

▪ Open the main document and if it is hidden, show the **Mail Merge** toolbar.

▪ Place the insertion point where the text is to appear in the main document.

▪ Click the **Insert Word Field** button then the **If ... Then ... Else** option.

▪ Enter your condition using the **Field name**, **Comparison** and **Compare to** lists.

▪ In the **Insert this text** box, enter the text that will be printed if the condition is satisfied.

▪ Use the **Otherwise insert this text** box to enter a text that will be printed if the condition is not satisfied.

*You cannot format your text when you enter it into the **Insert this text** or **Otherwise insert this text** boxes: this must be performed in the main document.*

Insert Word Field: IF

IF

Field name:	Comparison:	Compare to:
Title	Equal to	Mr

Insert this text:

Dear Sir

Otherwise insert this text:

Dear Madam

OK   Cancel

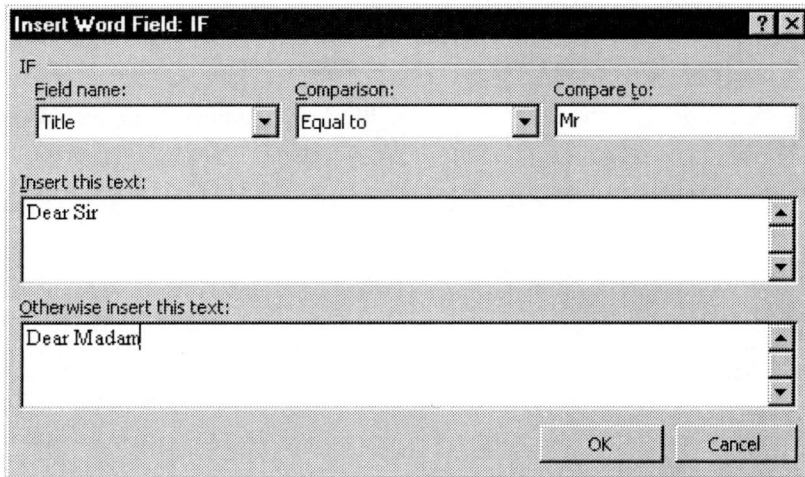

In this example, if the Title field contains the mention "Mr", the text "Dear Sir" will appear in the letter and if it contains another title, "Dear Madam" will appear.

▪ Click **OK**.

If the field code display is no longer active, display the codes by pressing [Alt] [F9] *to read what you have just created.*

For example: {IF{MERGEFIELDTitle} = "Mr" "Dear Sir" "Dear Madam"}.

▪ Save the main document and close it.

6 ▪ Sorting a list of data

▪ Open the main document and if it is hidden, show the **Mail Merge** toolbar.

▪ Click the [ ] tool button on the **Mail Merge** toolbar.

▪ Open the list associated with one of the fields then click the **(Advanced)** option.

▪ If necessary, click the **Sort Records** tab.

When the dialog box opens, you can see that you can sort by up to three fields.

* Open the **Sort by** list, click the name of the field and specify whether the records should be sorted in **Ascending** or **Descending** order.

* If several records are likely to have the same value, use the **Then by** lists to indicate a second or even a third field to sort by.

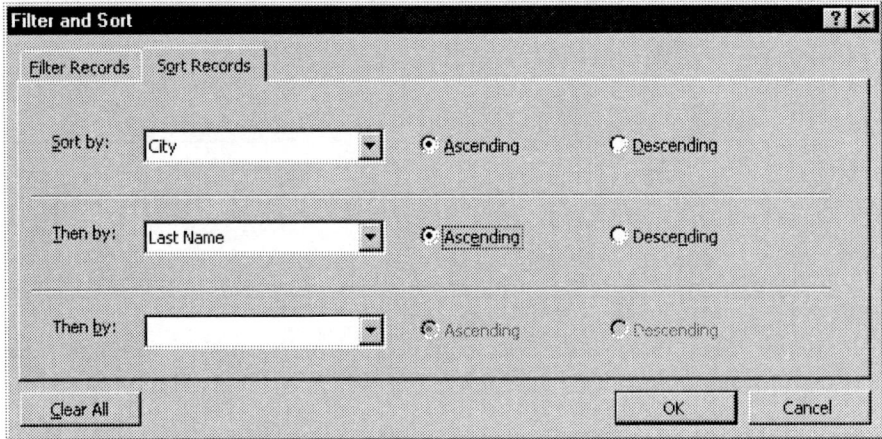

The records are sorted according to the first sort criterion. When this value is the same on more than one record (for example, the city is London on several records), the second sort criterion comes into effect (the records for London are then sorted by name) and so on.

* Click **OK**.

*The sorted list appears in the **Mail Merge Recipients** dialog box.*

* Click **OK**.

*You can set a single sort order for the list in the **Mail Merge Recipients** dialog box (click the ▣ tool button): click the name of the field by which you wish to sort and it will be sorted in ascending order. Click again to sort in descending order.*

⊞7 ▪ Creating mailing labels

▪ For the main document for your mailing labels, you can use an existing mailing label document from a previous merge or create a new blank document.

Whichever of these options you intend to use, start by clicking the ⬚ tool button on the **Standard** toolbar.

▪ **Tools - Letters and Mailings - Mail Merge Wizard**

▪ Activate the **Labels** option in the **Select document type** frame.

▪ Click the **Next: Starting document** link at the bottom of the task pane.

▪ In the **Select starting document** frame, select an option according to how you wish to make up your mailing labels:

Change document layout: the main document for the mail merge labels is the current document, in which you define the size of the mailing labels. To choose the size of the labels, click the **Label Options** link in the **Change document layout** frame and double-click the required **Product number**.

The *Details button in the Label Options dialog box can be used to customise the options of the selected label and the New Label button leads you to create a new custom label that will be added to the Product number list.*

Start from existing document: the main document for the mailing labels is based on an existing mail merge document (already containing mailing labels). If this document's name appears in the **Start from existing** list, select its name and click the **Open** button, otherwise select the **[More files...]** option. Click the **Open** button and select the file. A new **DocumentX** based on the selected mail merge document appears on the screen.

▪ Click the **Next: Select recipients** link to go to the next step.

The *Previous: Select document type link takes you back to the step before.*

▪ Activate one of the options in the **Select recipients** frame to choose a list of addressees:

Use an existing list: use to select a file or database containing the list of recipients. Click the **Browse** link in the **Use existing list** frame to select the file or database containing the names and addresses. If necessary, modify the contents of the file and click **OK**. If the selected list is no longer suitable, **Select a different list** by clicking this link.

If your data list is an Excel workbook (.xls) or an Access database (.mdb), Word will show you a dialog box when the file opens so you can choose the workbook sheet or the database table containing the data you need to use for the mailing labels.

Select from Outlook contacts: use to select the recipient list from an Outlook contacts folder. To do this, click the **Choose Contacts Folder** link in the **Select from Outlook contacts** frame, double-click the contacts folder containing the recipients' names, modify the list if necessary then click **OK**.

Type a new list: you enter the contents of a new mailing list (cf. Creating a list of data above).

▪ Click the **Next: Arrange your labels** link to go to the next step.

▪ Define how to set out the contents of the labels in the first label on the page. For each field you wish to insert, follow this procedure:

 - Place the insertion point where the contents of the label should print.

 - Click the **More items** link on the task pane, select the field concerned and click the **Insert** button. Click **Close**.

*The **Address block** link opens the **Insert Address Block** dialog box, where you can choose predefined formats for the name and address (these insert an **Address Block** field). The **Greeting line** link provides a dialog box with options for inserting an initial greeting in your letter (a **Greeting Line** field).*

▪ If necessary, apply formatting to the label's contents.

▪ Copy the layout of the first label onto the other labels on the page by clicking the **Update all labels** button in the **Replicate labels** frame.

▪ Click the **Next: Preview your labels** link to go to the next step.

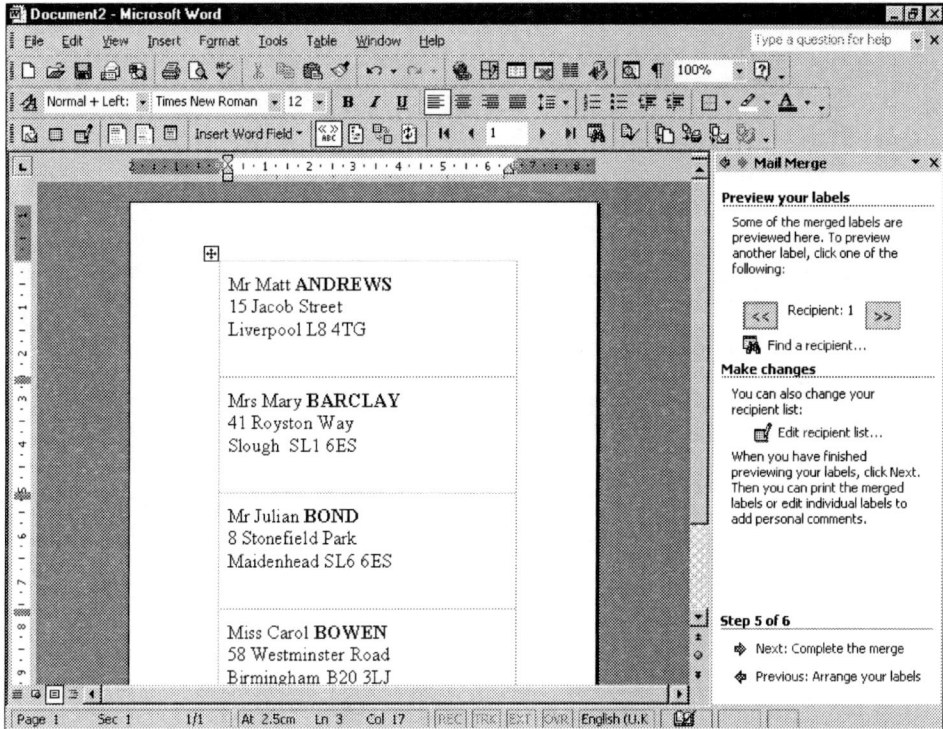

In the main document, you see a preview of the first page of labels.

» If you wish, use [Alt][F9] to toggle the display of field codes on or off.

» Use the [<<] and [>>] buttons in the **Preview your labels** frame to show the label for the previous or next record.

» Click the **Next: Complete the merge** link to go to the last step of the wizard.

» Click the **Print** link to merge to the printer and print your mailing labels or the **Edit individual labels** link to create the merged labels in a new document called **Labels** followed by a number.

* If you have chosen to **Edit individual labels**, specify which labels should be merged. To merge all the selected records in the list of data, activate the **All** option. To merge the records corresponding to the first page of labels, activate the **Current record** option. To limit the merge to certain selected records in the list of data, give the number of the first label required in the **From** box and the last in the **To** box. However, even if you do this, Word will always print a complete page of labels and may print records you did not request. For example, if you request records 5 to 15 and there are eight records to a page, records 5 to 12 will print on one page but 13 to 20 will print on the next as Word will complete the page it has started, so as to leave no blank labels.

* If you merge to a new document, make the required changes, print and/or save the document and close it.

* Save the main document and close it.

  If changes have been made to the list of data, Word prompts you to save them.

* If necessary, click **Yes** to save any changes made to the data list.

Below, you can see **Practice Exercise** 3.2. This exercise is made up of 7 steps. If you do not know how to do one of the steps, go back to the title that corresponds to that particular lesson. When you have finished, you can check your work by reading the **Solution** that follows.

Steps in the exercise that are likely to be tested on the exam are preceded by this symbol: ▯. However, it is a good idea to complete all the steps in the exercise, to ensure that you have understood all the points discussed in the lesson.

👉 **Practice Exercise 3.2**

▯ 1. Create a mail merge following the example below:

FLOR TOUR

«First_name» «Last_name»
«Address»
«City» «Postcode»

Re: Information
Ref.: INF/US

«Title» «Last_name»,

 Thank you for your request for more information about our holidays to the United States.

Please find enclosed our information pack, which details all the packages to the United States for the coming year.

Thank you again for your interest, and please do not hesitate to contact us if you have any further questions.

Mary Watts

North America Co-ordinator

- the main document is based on a document called **3-2 Form letter.doc** in the **MOUS Word 2002 Expert** folder.

- the list of data is called **3-2 Customers.doc** and is in the **MOUS Word 2002 Expert** folder.

- run the mail merge in a new document, check that the first few letters have been merged correctly then close the document without saving it.

Save the main document in the **MOUS Word 2002 Expert** folder, under the name **3-2 Information.doc**.

2. For the **3-2 Information.doc** main document (this is the active document), create the following list of data which you should save in the **MOUS Word 2002 Expert** folder as **3-2 Addresses.mdb**; the fields should appear in the order in which you enter the data.

Title	First Name	Last Name	Address	City	Postcode
Mr	John	Morrow	15 Crabtree Lane	Ipswich	IPS 450
Miss	Susan	Parker	2A Reland St	Marlow	MAR 550
Mrs	Tania	Baverstock	67 Milton Park	Dalby	DAL 990
Miss	Virginia	Davis	5 Freers Drive	Marlow	MAR 440
Mr	Ross	Chambers	88 Bluebell Drive	Blacktown	BLA 440
Miss	Maureen	Tully	454 Marine Drive	North Bay	NOR 660
Mr	Duncan	Holt	9 Hurst St	Roma Park	ROM 220
Mrs	Anne	Sutcliffe	69B Farley Rd	Nellington	NEL 440
Miss	Lea	Pearce	11 Forman St	Abbyville	ABB 330

3. Go to the data entry grid and make the following changes:

- add this record: **Mrs Sheila Barker, 17 Newton Road, Blacktown, BLA 440**.

- find the record for **Mr Holt** and delete it.

- Mrs Sutcliffe's address has changed to **23 Milehouse Park**; find her record and change the address.

4. Set criteria that will merge only the records referring to clients called **Miss** living in **Marlow**.
Run this mail merge in a new document; check the result of the merge then close the document without saving it. Finish by deleting all the criteria set and go to step **3** in the Mail Merge Wizard.

5. Remove the **Title** and **Last Name** fields in the greeting line and insert a field with a condition, so that when the value in the **Title** field is **Mr**, the text **Dear Sir** is printed and when the title is something else, **Dear Madam** is printed (make sure there is a space between the condition and the field).

Check the contents of the first few letters using step **5** (**Preview your letters**) in the Mail Merge Wizard.

6. Sort the list of data in ascending order by **City** then by **Last Name**. Save the changes made to the **3-2 Information.doc** main document then close it.

7. In a new document, create mailing labels for the addresses in the **3-2 Customers.doc** data list as shown below; use the **2160 MiniAddress** type of label and ensure the surnames appear in bold type:

```
«Title» «First_name» «Last_name»
«Address»
«City» «Postcode»
```

Merge the labels into a new document, check the result and close the document without saving it. Save the main document in the **MOUS Word 2002 Expert** folder as **3-2 Address labels.doc** then close it.

If you would like to practise these features more, on another document, you should work through Summary Exercise 3, on MAIL MERGE. You will find the summary exercises at the end of the book.

It is often possible to perform a task in several different ways, but here, only the easiest solution is presented. You can go back to the corresponding lesson if you want to see other techniques you could use.

Solution to Exercise 3.2

1. To create the mail merge described in step 1, make sure a new document is displayed on the screen then use the **Tools - Letters and Mailings - Mail Merge Wizard**.

   Activate the **Letters** option in the **Mail Merge** task pane then click the **Next: Starting document** link.

   Activate the **Start from existing document** option, make sure that the **More Files...)** option is active in the **Start from existing** frame and click the **Open** button. Select the **MOUS Word 2002 Expert** folder, choose the **3-2 Form letter.doc** document and click the **Open** button. Click the **Next: Select recipients** link to go to the next step.

   Activate the **Use an existing list** option then click the **Browse** button. Select the **MOUS Word 2002 Expert** folder, double-click the **3-2 Customers.doc** document then click the **OK** button on the **Mail Merge Recipients** dialog box. Next, click the **Next: Write your letter** link to go to the next step.

   To insert each field into the document as shown in step 1, proceed as follows:

   - place the insertion point where the field's contents should print.

   - click the **More items** link on the **Mail Merge** task pane.

   - select the field concerned.

   - click the **Insert** button and **Close**.

   Click the **Next: Preview your letters** link then the **Next: Complete the merge** link.

   To create the mail merge in a new document, click the **Edit individual letters** link, make sure the **All** option is active and click **OK**.

To check the result of the mail merge by looking at the first three letters, scroll down through the document.

To close the document without saving it, use the **File - Close** command and click **No** on the message that asks if you want to save your work.

To save the main document in the MOUS Word 2002 Expert folder, as 3-2 Information.doc, click the 🖫 tool button, select the **MOUS Word 2002 Expert** folder, type **3-2 Information.doc** in the **File name** text box then click the **Save** button.

2. To create the data list shown in step 2 for the 3-2 Information.doc document, go to step **3** of the Mail Merge Wizard by clicking the **Previous: Preview your letters**, **Previous: Write your letter** and **Previous: Select recipients** links in the **Mail Merge** task pane.
Activate the **Type a new list** option in the **Select recipients** frame and click the **Create** link.
Click the **Customize** button then delete the **Company Name, Address Line 1, Address Line 2, ZIP Code, State, Country, Home Phone, Work Phone** and **E-mail Address** fields. To delete each field, select it in the **Field Names** list, click the **Delete** button and click **Yes** to confirm the deletion.

To create an **Address** field, click the **Add** button, type **Address** in the **Type a name for your field** box and click **OK**.

To create a **Postcode** field, click the **Add** button, type **Postcode** in the **Type a name for your field** box and click **OK**.

To make the fields appear in the order in which the data should be entered, select the **Address** field and click the **Move Up** button twice.
Click **OK**.

To enter the records in the data list as shown in the table in step 2, click the cell in the **Title** field and enter the data for each record in the correct boxes, using the 🔄 key to go to the next field or [Shift] 🔄 to go back one field. After you have filled in the last field of the current record, click the **New Entry** button to start another record.

When you have entered all the records, click the **Close** button. Select the **MOUS Word 2002 Expert** folder, enter **3-2 Addresses** in the **File name** box and click the **Save** button.

To finish, click **OK** on the **Mail Merge Recipients** dialog box.

3. To go to the data entry grid, show the **Mail Merge** toolbar if it is not visible, using the **View - Toolbars - Mail Merge** command. Click the 🖳 tool button then click the **Edit** button.

To add a record for Sheila Barker, click the **New Entry** button and enter the new record as shown below:

C:\MOUS Word 2002 Expert\3-2 Addresses.mdb	? X

Enter Address information	
Title	Mrs
First Name	Sheila
Last Name	Barker
Address	17 Newton Rd
City	Blacktown
Postcode	BLA 440

New Entry	Delete Entry	Find Entry ...	Filter and Sort...	Customize...

View Entries

View Entry Number	First	Previous	11	Next	Last

Total entries in list   11

Close

To look for the record concerning Mr Holt, click the **First** button to return to the first record then click the **Find Entry** button. Type **Holt** in the **Find** box then select **Last Name** in the **This field** list. Click the **Find Next** button then click **Cancel**.

To delete the record concerning Mr Holt, click the **Delete Entry** button then click **Yes** to confirm the deletion.

To change the record concerning Mrs Sutcliffe, click the **Find Entry** button, type **Sutcliffe** in the **Find** box, select **Last Name** in the **This field** list, click **Find Next** then **Cancel**. Select the contents of the **Address** field, press the ⌊Del⌋ key and enter the text **23 Milehouse Park**.
Click the **Close** button then click **OK** on the **Mail Merge Recipients** dialog box.

4. To set criteria that will merge only the records referring to female clients called Miss living in Marlow, start by displaying the **Mail Merge** toolbar, if it is hidden and click the ⊞ tool button.
Open the list attached to any field (for example, on the **Last Name** field), click the **(Advanced...)** option and if necessary, click the **Filter Records** tab.
Fill in the dialog box as shown below:

Filter and Sort			? X
Filter Records	Sort Records		
	Field:	Comparison:	Compare to:
	Title	Equal to	Miss
And	City	Equal to	Marlow
And			
Clear All		OK	Cancel

Click **OK** twice.

To run the merge in a new document, check the result then close the document without saving it, go to step **6** in the Mail Merge Wizard by clicking in succession the **Next: Write your letter**, **Next: Preview your letters** then the **Next: Complete the merge** links. Click the **Edit individual letters** link, make sure the **All** option is active then click **OK**. Scroll through the document to check the result of the merge then close the new document without saving it (use the **File - Close** command and click **No** on the message that asks if you want to save).

To delete all the set criteria, click the [tool] tool button, open the list attached to any field (for example, on the **Last Name** field), click the **(Advanced...)** option and if necessary, click the **Filter Records** tab. Click the **Clear All** button and click **OK** twice.

To go to step 3 on the Mail Merge Wizard, click the **Previous: Preview your letters**, **Previous: Write your letter** and **Previous: Select recipients** links in the **Mail Merge** task pane.

5. To remove the Title and Last Name fields in the greeting line and insert a field with a condition line, start by selecting the **Title** and **Last Name** fields on the greeting line and press the [Del] key. If it is hidden, display the **Mail Merge** toolbar and click the **Insert Word Field** list. Choose the **If ... Then ... Else ...** option and complete the dialog box as shown below:

Click **OK**.

To check the contents of the first few letters in step **5** of the Mail Merge Wizard, click the **Next: Write your letter** and **Next: Preview your letters** links. Scroll through the first six letters with the ▨ button that appears in the **Preview your letters** frame on the **Mail Merge** task pane.

6. To sort the list by **City** then by **Last Name**, click the ▨ tool button on the **Mail Merge** toolbar.
   Open the list attached to any field (for example, on the **Last Name** field), click the **(Advanced...)** option and if necessary, click the **Sort Records** tab. Fill in the **Filter and Sort** dialog box as shown here:

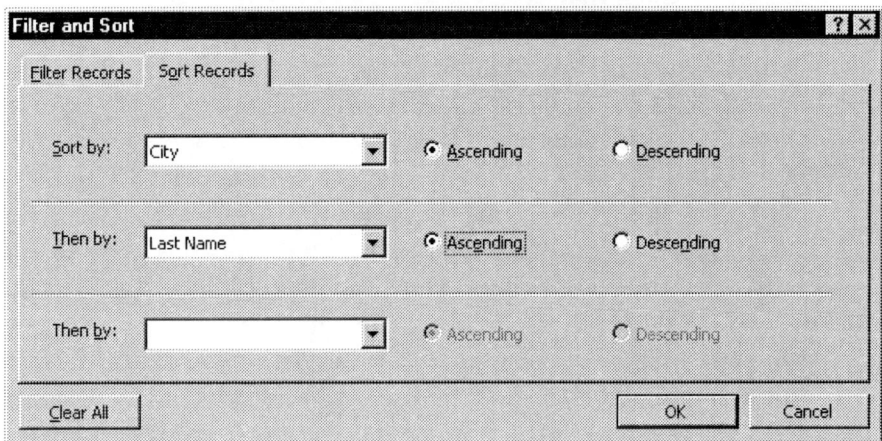

Filter and Sort		? ✕
Filter Records ⎸ Sort Records ⎸		
Sort by: ⎸City ▾⎸	⦿ Ascending	○ Descending
Then by: ⎸Last Name ▾⎸	⦿ Ascending	○ Descending
Then by: ⎸ ▾⎸	⦾ Ascending	○ Descending
Clear All	OK	Cancel

Click **OK** twice.

To save the changes made to the 3-2 Information.doc document, click the ▨ tool button on the **Standard** toolbar.

To close the 3-2 Information.doc main document, use the **File - Close** command.

7. To create mailing labels in a new document for the addresses in the 3-2 Customers.doc document, as shown in step 7, click the ▯ tool button to create a new document then use the **Tools - Letters and Mailings - Mail Merge Wizard** command.

Activate the **Labels** option in the **Mail Merge** task pane then click the **Next: Starting document** link.

Leave the **Change document layout** option, click the **Label options** link then double-click the **2160 Mini-Address** reference in the **Product number** list. Click the **Next: Select recipients** link to go to the next step.

Activate the **Use an existing list** option then click the **Browse** button. Select the **MOUS Word 2002 Expert** folder, double-click the **3-2 Customers.doc** file then click **OK** on the **Mail Merge Recipients** dialog box. Click the **Next: Arrange your labels** link.

Place the insertion point on the first paragraph of the first label on the page. Click the **More items** link, select the **Title** field then click **Insert** and **Close**. Press the `Space` bar, click the **More items** link, select the **First_name** field then click **Insert** and **Close**. Press the `Space` bar, click the **More items** link, select the **Last_name** field then click **Insert** and **Close**. Press the ↵ key, click the **More items** link, select the **Address** field then click **Insert** and **Close**. Press the ↵ key, click the **More items** link, select the **City** field then click **Insert** and **Close**. Press the `Space` bar, click the **More items** link, select the **Postcode** field then click **Insert** and **Close**.

To make the last name appear in bold type on each label, select the **Last_name** field (including the << and >> symbols) in the first label on the page then click the **B** tool button on the **Formatting** toolbar.

Click the **Update all labels** button that appears at the bottom of the **Mail Merge** task pane then click the **Next: Preview your labels** and **Next: Complete the merge** links.

To run the merge in a new document, click the **Edit individual labels** link, make sure the **All** option is active and click **OK**.

To see the merge result, scroll down through the document.

To close the new document without saving it, use the **File - Close** command and click **No** on the message that asks if you want to save.

To save the changes made to the main label document, into the MOUS Word 2002 Expert folder as 3-2 Address labels.doc, click the tool button, select the **MOUS Word 2002 Expert** folder if necessary then enter **3-2 Address labels** in the **File name** box and click the **Save** button.

To close the main label document, use the **File - Close** command.

OTHER ADVANCED FUNCTIONS
Lesson 4.1: Macros

1 ▪ Creating a macro

A macro saves a series of commands as a single command in order to automate your work in Word. A macro is written in the Visual Basic programming language. Macros are stored in the document or in a document template.

▪ If you wish to save the macro in a particular document or template, open that document (for a template you can open a document based on that template). If no document is open, the macro will be saved in the Normal.dot template.

▪ **Tools - Macro - Record New Macro**

▪ Enter the **Macro name** in the appropriate text box.

▪ In the **Store macro in** list, give the name of the document or template in which the macro should be saved.

*Macros can be saved in the standard template (**All Documents (Normal.dot)**), in the active document or in the template on which the active document is based.*

▪ If you wish, enter a **Description**.

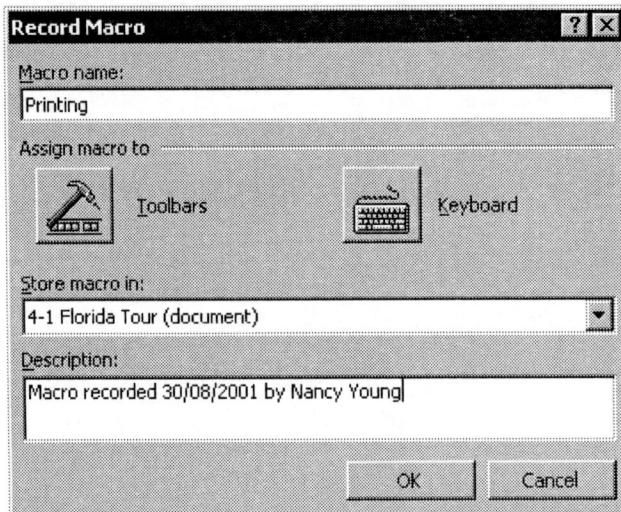

▪ To run your macro quickly and easily, you can associate it with a tool button or a keyboard shortcut by clicking one of these buttons:

Toolbars   using the **Commands** frame under the **Commands** tab, drag the macro icon onto the required toolbar to create a button associated with the macro.

Keyboard   use to give a keyboard shortcut to your macro.

▪ Click **OK**.

*The macro **Stop Recording** toolbar appears and the letters **REC** appear in bold on the status bar.*

▪ Make all the actions you wish the macro to record.

▪ If you want to perform an action that should not be recorded, pause the recording by clicking the ▐▌● tool button on the **Stop Recording** toolbar. Click this button again to resume recording.

▪ When you have performed all the necessary actions, click the ■ tool button on the **Stop Recording** toolbar.

*The letters **REC** appear once again in grey on the status bar.*

▪ Running a macro

▪ **Tools - Macro - Macros** or Alt F8

*The **Macros** dialog box appears and lists all the macros in the template.*

▪ If required, open the **Macros in** list to select the document or template containing the macro you wish to run.

▪ Double-click the **Macro name** you want to run or select the name and click the **Run** button.

If you associated a tool button or shortcut keys with the macro, you can run it by clicking its tool button or pressing the shortcut keys.

3 ▪ Modifying a macro

- **Tools - Macro - Macros** or [Alt] [F8]
- Select the **Macro name** you wish to modify.
- Click the **Edit** button.

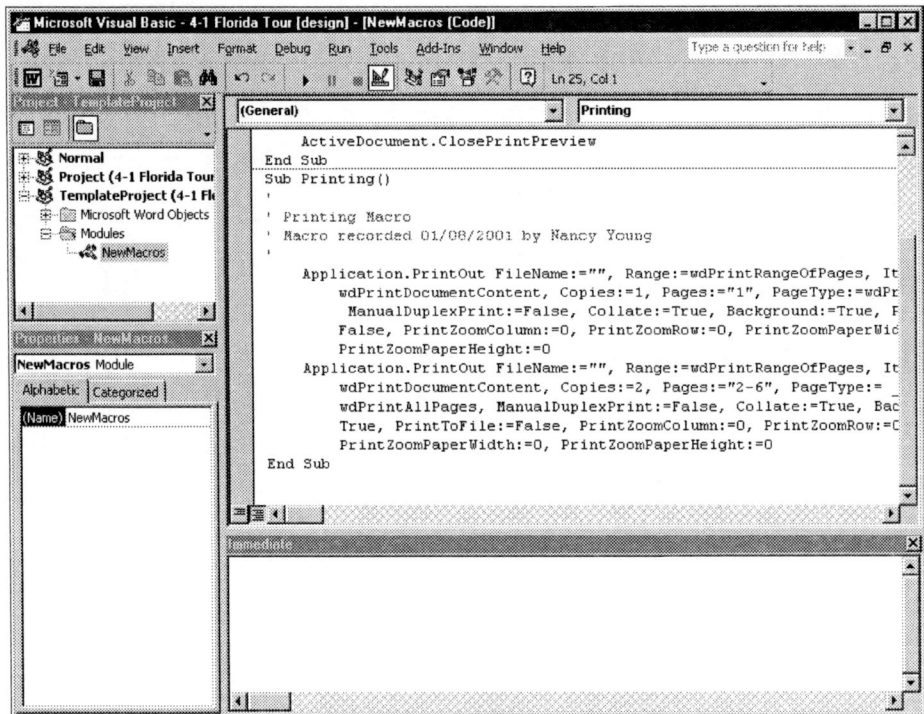

The Microsoft Visual Basic application window shows how the macros have been recorded in the Visual Basic programming language.

- Make any required changes.
- Leave the Microsoft Visual Basic application with **File - Close and Return to Microsoft Word** or [Alt] Q.

4 ▪ Deleting a macro

▪ **Tools - Macro - Macros** or `Alt` `F8`

▪ If required, open the **Macros in** list to select the document or template containing the macro you wish to delete.

▪ Select the **Macro name** you want to delete.

▪ Click the **Delete** button.

▪ Confirm the deletion by clicking **Yes**.

▪ Click the **Close** button.

5 ▪ Managing a macro project

*The different macros that you save in a template or document are regrouped in a macro known as a **macro project**, called **NewMacros** by default.*

Going to the Organizer dialog box

▪ If it is not open, open the document or template that contains the macro project you want to change.

▪ **Tools - Macro - Macros** or `Alt` `F8`

▪ Click the **Organizer** button.

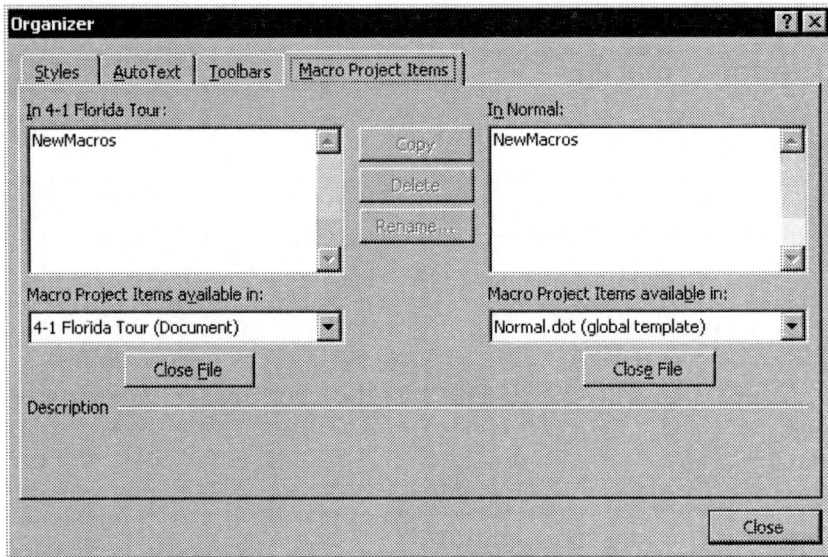

The ***Organizer*** dialog box opens with the ***Macro Project Items*** tab active. In the list on the left, Word lists the macro projects in the active document and, on the right, the macro projects in the global template (Normal.dot).

* Open one of the **Macro Project Items available in** drop-down lists to see the macro projects in the current template or document.

* To see a template other than **Normal.dot**, click the **Close File** button under the list on the right then click the **Open File** button that replaces it and select the template you require.

Copying a macro project

* Go into the **Organizer** dialog box.

* If necessary, select the source and destination templates. To do this, click the **Close File** button then open the **Macro Project Items available in** drop-down list.

* In one of the lists, select the macro project(s) you want to copy.

* Click the **Copy** button.

The macro project is copied into the other template instantly.

* Click the **Close** button.

📄 *To copy a single macro, edit it and use the features in Visual Basic.*

Renaming/deleting a macro project

* Go into the **Organizer** dialog box.
* If necessary, select the source template in one of the **Macro Project Items available in** lists.
* Select the macro project you wish to rename or delete.
* To rename a macro project, click the **Rename** button, enter the new name and click **OK**.
* To delete a macro project, click the **Delete** button and confirm the deletion by clicking **Yes**.
* Close the **Organizer** dialog box by clicking its **Close** button.

Below, you can see **Practice Exercise** 4.1. This exercise is made up of 5 steps. If you do not know how to do one of the steps, go back to the title that corresponds to that particular lesson. When you have finished, you can check your work by reading the **Solution** that follows.

Steps in the exercise that are likely to be tested on the exam are preceded by this symbol: 📖. However, it is a good idea to complete all the steps in the exercise, to ensure that you have understood all the points discussed in the lesson.

☞ Practice Exercise 4.1

To work on practice exercise 4.1, open the ***4-1 Florida Tour.doc*** *document, located in the* ***MOUS Word 2002 Expert*** *folder.*

📖 1. Create a macro that will print one copy of the first page of the document and two copies of the other pages. Call this macro **Printing** and save it in the **4-1 Florida Tour.doc** document.

📖 2. Run the macro you have just recorded (**Printing**) in the **4-1 Florida Tour.doc** document.

📖 3. Modify the **Printing** macro so three copies of the first page are printed.

4. Delete the macro called **PrintPrev**, which is saved in the **4-1 Florida Tour.doc** document.

5. Rename the macro project which is currently called "NewMacros" and which is in the **4-1 Florida Tour.doc** document: call the macro **FloridaMacro.**
Finish by closing the **4-1 Florida Tour.doc** document without saving the changes you have made.

If you would like to practise these features more, on another document, you should work through Summary Exercise 4, on OTHER ADVANCED FUNCTIONS. You will find the summary exercises at the end of the book.

It is often possible to perform a task in several different ways, but here, only the easiest solution is presented. You can go back to the corresponding lesson if you want to see other techniques you could use.

Solution to Exercise 4.1

1. To create a macro that will print one copy of the first page of the document and two copies of the other pages, use the **Tools - Macro - Record New Macro** command.
   In the **Macro name** box, type **Printing**. In the **Store macro in** list, choose **4-1 Florida Tour.doc** document then click **OK**.

   Carry out the following actions:
   File - Print; activate the **Pages** option and enter **1** in the attached text box; click **OK**.
   File - Print; enter **2-6** in the **Pages** text box, enter **2** in the **Number of copies** text box and click **OK**.

   Click the ▪ tool button on the **Stop** toolbar to stop recording the macro.

2. To run the macro you have just recorded in the **4-1 Florida Tour.doc** document, use the **Tools - Macro - Macros** command.
   If necessary, choose the **4-1 Florida Tour.doc (document)** option in the **Macros in** list.
   Select the **Printing** macro then click the **Run** button.

3. To modify the "Printing" macro so three copies of the first page are printed, use the **Tools - Macro - Macros** command, select the **Printing** macro and click the **Edit** button.

   In the Microsoft Visual Basic window, change the **Copies:=1** instruction into **Copies:=3**.
   Leave the Microsoft Visual Basic application with the **File - Close and Return to Microsoft Word** command.

4. To delete the "PrintPrev" macro, use the **Tools - Macro - Macros** command. Open the **Macros in** list and choose **4-1 Florida Tour.doc (document)**. Select the **PrintPrev** macro then click the **Delete** button. Click **Yes** to confirm the deletion then click the **Close** button.

5. To rename the macro project, which is currently called "NewMacros" in the 4-1 Florida Tour.doc document, use the **Tools - Macro - Macros** command and click the **Organizer** button.
Select the **NewMacros** project in the **In 4-1 Florida Tour** box, click the **Rename** button, type **FloridaMacro** then click **OK** and **Close**.

To close the 4-1 Florida Tour.doc document without saving the changes made, use the **File - Close** command and click **No** on any messages that ask if you want to save your changes.

OTHER ADVANCED FUNCTIONS
Lesson 4.2: Toolbars

1 ▪ Customising a toolbar

Opening the Customize dialog box

▪ Go into the template concerned.

▪ Display the toolbar you wish to customise, with the **View - Toolbars** command.

▪ **View - Toolbars - Customize**

*You can also access this dialog box with the **Tools - Customize** command or by right-clicking any toolbar and choosing the **Customize** option.*

Removing a tool button

▪ Make sure that the bar from which you want to delete a tool button is displayed.

▪ Open the **Customize** dialog box.

▪ If necessary, click the **Commands** tab and open the **Save in** list to choose the document or template containing the tool you want to delete.

▪ On the toolbar itself, point to the tool button you want to remove and drag it off the bar.

Once you release the mouse button, the tool button disappears.

▪ Click the **Close** button on the **Customize** dialog box.

Adding a tool button

▪ Open the **Customize** dialog box.

▪ Click the **Commands** tab.

▪ In the **Save in** list, choose the document or template in which you want to add the tool button to the toolbar.

▪ Select the category of the tool in the **Categories** box.

▪ In the **Commands** list, click the row of the command you wish to add.

Customize dialog box:

Customize `? X`

Tool**b**ars | **C**ommands | **O**ptions

To add a command to a toolbar: select a category and drag the
command out of this dialog box to a toolbar.

Categori**e**s:
```
File
Edit
View
Insert
Format
Tools
Table
Web
Window and Help
Drawing
```

Comman**d**s:
- Show Field Shading
- Full Screen
- Magnifier
- Zoom 100%
- Fit To Window

Selected command:

[Descri**p**tion] [Modify Selection ▼]

[?] **S**ave in: [4-2 Florida Tour.doc ▼] [**K**eyboard...] [Close]

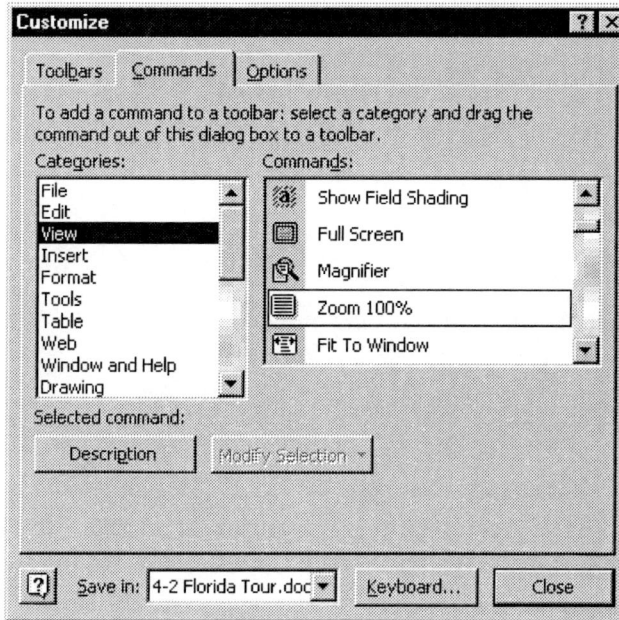

Click the **Description** button to check what the tool does.

» Drag the button from the dialog box directly onto the appropriate toolbar in the Word window.

» Choose what should be displayed with the **Modify Selection** button.

» Click the **Close** button on the **Customize** dialog box.

You can also add or remove tool buttons by clicking the small black arrow visible at the very right of most toolbars then choosing **Add or Remove Buttons**.

Customising the look of a tool button

* Open the **Customize** dialog box and click the **Commands** tab.

* On the toolbar, in the Word window, click the button you wish to customise.

* Click the **Modify Selection** button.

* Use the different options in this menu to change the presentation of the tool button.

* Click the **Close** button on the **Customize** dialog box.

> To restore the original toolbars for a document or template, open that document, template or a document that is based on that template then use the **Tools - Customize** command and click the **Toolbars** tab. Click the name of the toolbar concerned then click the **Reset** button. In the dialog box that appears, select the name of the document or template containing the toolbar you wish to restore and click **OK**.

2 ▪ Creating/deleting a custom toolbar

* Open the template or document in which you wish to make the toolbar available.

* **View - Toolbars - Customize**

* Click the **Toolbars** tab then the **New** button.

* Enter the **Toolbar name** for the bar you are creating.

New Toolbar ? ✕

Toolbar name:

Zoom

Make toolbar available to:

4-2 Florida Tour.doc ▼

OK   Cancel

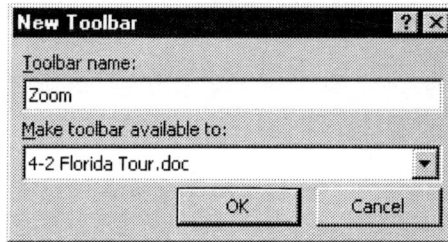

- In the **Make toolbar available to** text box, select the document or template concerned.

- Click **OK**.

  *The name of your new toolbar appears at the bottom of the **Toolbars** list in the **Customize** dialog box. The new toolbar itself appears on the screen as a floating toolbar.*

- Add all the tool buttons you require using the lists under the **Commands** tab.

- Click the **Close** button.

- If you wish, dock the new toolbar by double-clicking its title bar.

  *To delete a custom toolbar, click its name on the **Toolbars** page of the **Customize** dialog box then click **Delete**.*

3 ▪ Customising menus

Deleting a menu/menu option

- Open the template or document concerned then open the **Customize** dialog box with **Tools - Customize**.

- If necessary, click the **Commands** tab.

- To delete a menu option, open the menu in the menu bar on the application window. Point to the menu or option name that you want to remove and drag it clear of any menu.

- Close the **Customize** dialog box by clicking the **Close** button.

Adding an option to a menu

⊛ Open the document or template concerned then open the **Customize** dialog box (**Tools - Customize**).

⊛ Click the **Commands** tab.

⊛ Open the menu concerned on the menu bar on the application window.

⊛ Select the category of the option you want to add in the **Categories** box.

⊛ In the **Commands** list, click the option you wish to add.

⊛ Drag it into the required position on the open menu in the Word application window.

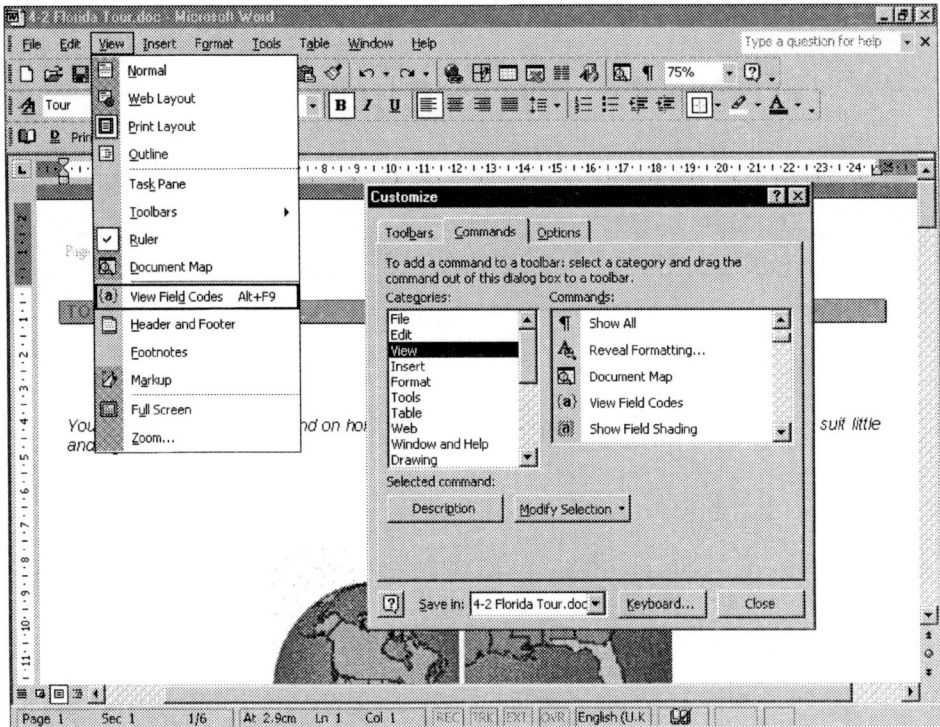

⊛ Click the **Close** button on the **Customize** dialog box.

Renaming a menu or an option

❋ Open the template or document concerned then open the **Customize** dialog box with **Tools - Customize**.

❋ If necessary, click the **Commands** tab.

❋ Click the menu or option you wish to rename on the menu bar on the application window.

❋ Click the **Modify Selection** button on the **Customize** dialog box.

❋ Type the new name into the **Name** text box (type an **&** character in front of the letter which will appear underlined).

❋ Press the ⏎ key.

❋ Close the **Customize** dialog box by clicking **Close**.

Adding a new menu

❋ Open the template or document concerned, then open the **Customize** dialog box with **Tools - Customize**.

❋ If necessary, click the **Commands** tab then choose the **New Menu** category.

❋ Drag the **New Menu** name from the **Commands** list onto the correct position on the menu bar.

❋ Use the **Modify Selection** button to give the new menu a name.

❋ Click the name of the new menu to open it. Add the options of your choice.

❋ In the **Save in** list, check the template or document name then click the **Close** button.

Below, you can see **Practice Exercise** 4.2. This exercise is made up of 3 steps. If you do not know how to do one of the steps, go back to the title that corresponds to that particular lesson. When you have finished, you can check your work by reading the **Solution** that follows.

All the parts of this exercise are likely to be tested on the MOUS exam.

☞ Practice Exercise 4.2

*To work on practice exercise 4.2, open the **4-2 Florida Tour.doc** document, located in the **MOUS Word 2002 Expert** folder.*

1. Show the custom toolbar called **Florida** and customise it as follows:
   - delete the 🔲 tool button.
   - change the tool button text "Project.NewMacros.Printing" to **Printing**.

2. Create a toolbar called **Zoom** and save it in the **4-2 Florida Tour.doc** document. Add these tools to it: 🔲, 🔲 and 🔲, which can be found in the **View** category.

3. Customise the menus in the **4-2 Florida Tour.doc** document, following the instructions below:
   - Delete the **Cut**, **Copy** and **Paste** options from the **Edit** menu.
   - Add the **View Field Codes** option (**View** category) above the **Header and Footer** option in the **View** menu.
   - Rename the **View Field Codes** option in the **View** menu as **Show/Hide Field Codes**.
   Save the changes made to the document then close it.

If you would like to practise these features more, on another document, you should work through Summary Exercise 4, on OTHER ADVANCED FUNCTIONS. You will find the summary exercises at the end of the book.

It is often possible to perform a task in several different ways, but here, only the easiest solution is presented. You can go back to the corresponding lesson if you want to see other techniques you could use.

Solution to Exercise 4.2

1. To show the custom toolbar called "Florida", use the **View - Toolbars - Florida** command. To customise this toolbar, use **View - Toolbars - Customize**.

   To delete the 🔳 tool button, drag it from the **Florida** toolbar away from any toolbar.

   To change the tool button text "Project.NewMacros.Printing" to "Printing", click the **Commands** tab.
   Click the button concerned on the **Florida** toolbar then click the **Modify Selection** button in the **Customize** dialog box.
   Select whatever is in the **Name** box and type **Printing** then press the ⏎ key.

   To close the **Customize** dialog box, click the **Close** button.

2. To create a toolbar called "Zoom" and save it in the 4-2 Florida Tour.doc document, use the **View - Toolbars - Customize** command. Click the **New** button on the **Toolbars** page.
   Type **Zoom** in the **Toolbar name** box and select **4-2 Florida Tour.doc** in the **Make toolbar available to** drop-down list.
   Click **OK**.

To add the ▤, ▦ and ▣ tool buttons, click the **Commands** tab and select **View** in the **Categories** list.

In the **Commands** list, click the **Zoom 100 %** command and drag it to the **Zoom** toolbar. Do the same thing for the **Fit To Window** and **One Page** commands.

Click the **Close** button on the **Customize** dialog box.

3. To customise the menus in the 4-2 Florida Tour.doc document, following the instructions in step 3, activate the **Tools - Customize** command and if necessary, select **4-2 Florida Tour.doc** in the **Save in** list, under the **Commands** tab.

For each option (**Cut**, **Copy** and **Paste**) that you want to delete from the **Edit** menu, click the **Edit** menu to open it. Drag each option concerned clear of the menu and clear of any toolbar.

To add the View Field Codes option above the Header and Footer option in the View menu, click **View** in the **Categories** list, under the **Commands** tab. Select the **View Field Codes** option in the **Commands** list then drag it above the **Header and Footer** option on the **View** menu.

To rename the View Field Codes option in the View menu as Show/Hide Field Codes, make sure the **View Field Codes** option is selected in the **View** menu then click the **Modify Selection** button in the **Customize** dialog box (**Commands** tab) In the **Name** box, delete the word **View** and type **Show** then press the / key (on the number pad). Type **Hide** then press the ↵ key.

Click the **Close** button on the **Customize** dialog box.

To save the changes made to the 4-2 Florida Tour.doc document, click the 🖬 tool button.

To close the 4-2 Florida Tour.doc document, use **File - Close**.

OTHER ADVANCED FUNCTIONS
Lesson 4.3: Smart tags

OTHER ADVANCED FUNCTIONS
Lesson 4.3: Smart tags

1 ▪ Using smart tags

*While you are typing in a Word document, a dotted purple line may appear beneath certain types of text. This indicator means that there is a **smart tag** associated with that particular item of text.*

Smart tags can be used to perform certain actions within Word more rapidly than ever before. The actions proposed by each smart tag depend on the type of data that Word recognises. For example, Sandra Reid (or Sandra REID) is recognised by Word as a "person name" smart tag. The associated actions enable you to open that person's contact file, if there is one, send that person an e-mail, if he/she has an e-mail address, set up a meeting, add that person's name to your contacts or even insert that person's address in your Word document, if it can be found in your list of contacts!

※ Point to the text that is underlined in purple to make the **Smart Tag Actions** button ⓘ appear.

※ Click the ⓘ button to see the list of actions associated with this type of data.

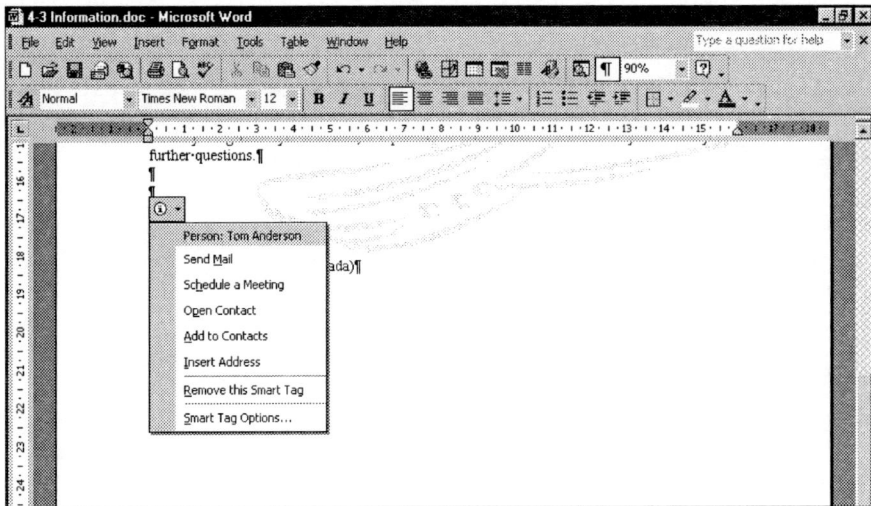

The text selected in this example is Tom Anderson; the list that opens from the ⓘ button hides the selected text.

» Click the name of the action you wish to carry out.

📄 *Smart tags are not available in a document that has been protected as a form.*

2 ▪ Managing smart tags

» **Tools - AutoCorrect Options**
» Click the **Smart Tags** tab.

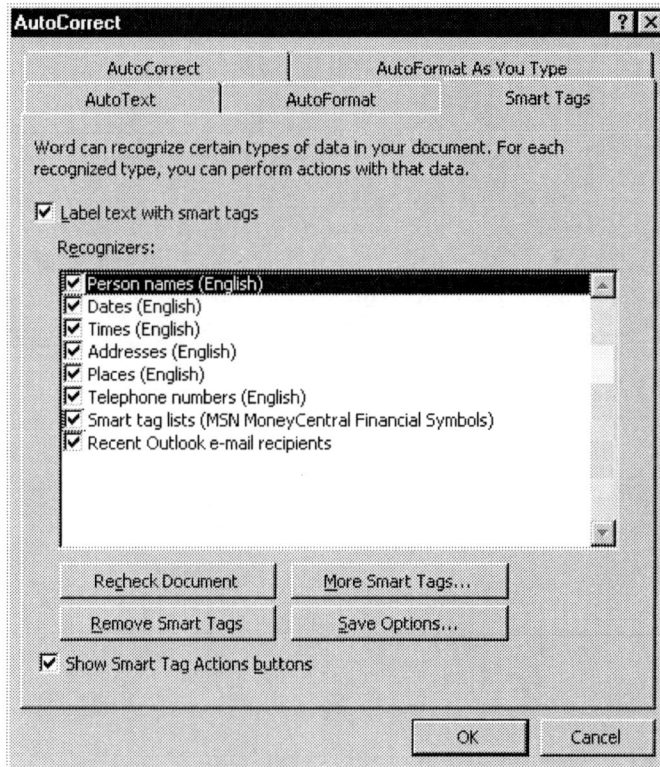

- To activate or deactivate smart tags, tick or deactivate the **Label text with smart tags** option.

- To choose what type of data Word should recognise and label with smart tags, activate or deactivate the options in the **Recognizers** list.

  *If the list of the type of data Word should recognise has been changed, you can apply your new choices to the active document by clicking the **Recheck Document** button.*

- To **Show Smart Tag Actions buttons** (⬚) in the document, make sure the corresponding option is ticked, otherwise remove the tick to hide these buttons. If you hide the buttons, you can no longer perform the actions.

- To save the smart tags when you save the document, click the **Save Options** button and activate the **Embed smart tags** option (or deactivate if you do not wish to save them). Click **OK**.

- Click **OK**.

  *You can show or hide the smart tag indicators (the dotted purple lines) by activating or deactivating the **Smart tags** option in the **Options** dialog box (**Tools - Options - View** tab). Hiding the indicators does not stop you using the smart tags feature. When you place the pointer over recognised text (such as a person's name) the **Smart Tag Actions** button still appears.*

  *Smart tags can be saved in an e-mail message so the message recipient can also use them. If you want to do this, make sure the **Save smart tags in e-mail** option is active in the **E-mail Options** dialog box (**Tools - Options - General** tab - **E-mail Options** button - **General** tab).*

  *You can download new smart tags from Web sites to add to those already installed with the Microsoft Word application. To do this, open the **AutoCorrect** dialog box (**Tools - AutoCorrect Options - Smart Tags** tab) and click the **More Smart Tags** button. In the Web page that appears, click the link that corresponds to the category that interests you then click the link to download the required smart tag application.*

3 ▪ Deleting smart tags

▪ To delete a smart tag from a text, point to the text until the **Smart Tag Actions** button ⓘ appears, click the ⓘ button and choose the **Remove this Smart Tag** option.

▪ To remove all the smart tags from the current document, click the **Remove Smart Tags** button on the **AutoCorrect** dialog box (**Tools - AutoCorrect Options - Smart Tags** tab).

The following error message appears on the screen:

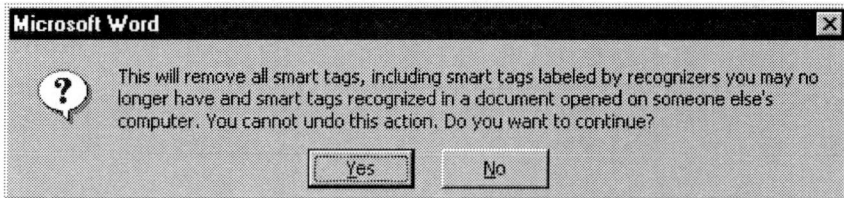

Microsoft Word	✕
❓ This will remove all smart tags, including smart tags labeled by recognizers you may no longer have and smart tags recognized in a document opened on someone else's computer. You cannot undo this action. Do you want to continue?	
[Yes] [No]	

▪ Click **Yes** then click **OK** on the message informing you that the smart tags have been deleted.

Below, you can see **Practice Exercise** 4.3. This exercise is made up of 3 steps. If you do not know how to do one of the steps, go back to the title that corresponds to that particular lesson. When you have finished, you can check your work by reading the **Solution** that follows.

☞ **Practice Exercise 4.3**

*To work on practice exercise 4.3, open the **4-3 Information.doc** document, located in the **MOUS Word 2002 Expert** folder.*

1. To work on this step of the exercise, you must have the Microsoft Outlook application installed on your computer.
   Enter the name **Tom Anderson** in the third last paragraph of the document and place the insertion point in the **Customer Service** paragraph. Use a smart tag action from the smart tag that appears by the name **Tom Anderson** to add this name to your list of contacts. Before saving the contact, add the following information:
   Company: Flor Tour
   Address (Business): 14 High Street, Westport WES 550
   Business Phone: 0155 777 8899
   E-mail: tanderson@flortour.com

2. Modify the smart tag options so that Microsoft Word recognises and assigns smart tags to every data type.

3. Delete the smart tag associated with the name **Helena Brewster** that appears above the letter's address at the top of the document.
   Finish by saving the changes made to the **4-3 Information.doc** document then close it.

If you would like to practise these features more, on another document, you should work through Summary Exercise 4, on OTHER ADVANCED FUNCTIONS. You will find the summary exercises at the end of the book.

It is often possible to perform a task in several different ways, but here, only the easiest solution is presented. You can go back to the corresponding lesson if you want to see other techniques you could use.

Solution to Exercise 4-3

1. To enter the name Tom Anderson in the third last paragraph of the document (this leaves one paragraph between his name and his job title), place the insertion point in the third last paragraph and type **Tom Anderson**.
   To place the insertion point in the paragraph starting "Customer Service", click any word in this paragraph.

   To use one of the smart tag actions offered for the name "Tom Anderson" and add this name to your Outlook contacts, click the name **Tom Anderson** so the ⓘ button appears then click this button. Click the **Add to Contacts** option.

   To add the information described in step 1 of the exercise, click the **Company** text box in the **Contact** dialog box and type **FLOR TOUR**. Click the **Address** button and in the **Street** box, type **14 High Street**, in the **City** box, type **Westport** and in the **ZIP/Postal Code** box, type **WES 550**. Click **OK**. Click the **Business** text box (next to the telephone icon) and type **0155 777 8899**. Click the **E-mail** box and enter :
   tanderson@flortour .com.

   To create the contact, click the 🖫 Save and Close button.

2. To modify the smart tag options so that Microsoft Word recognises and assigns smart tags to every data type, use the **Tools - AutoCorrect Options** command and click the **Smart Tags** tab on the **AutoCorrect** dialog box.
   Tick every check box in the **Recognizers** list then click **OK**.

3. To delete the smart tag associated with the name **Helena Brewster** that appears above the letter's address at the top of the document, click the name **Helena Brewster** so the ⓘ button appears. Click the ⓘ button then the **Remove this Smart Tag** option.

   To save the changes made to the 4-3 Information.doc document, click the 🖫 tool button.

   Use **File - Close** to close the 4-3 Information.doc document.

OTHER ADVANCED FUNCTIONS
Lesson 4.4: Workgroups

▤1 ▪ Tracking changes made to a document by other users

When several users work independently on the same document, they usually work on copies of that document. These copies can later be merged to form a single document.

Making a document available to several users

Before making one or more copies of a document, you must configure it so you can track the changes made to it.

⁕ Open the document that you wish to make available to several users.

⁕ **Tools - Track Changes** or `Ctrl` `Shift` **E**

*You can also activate tracking by clicking the **Track Changes** tool button* ▤ *on the **Reviewing** toolbar if that toolbar is on the screen.*

*If the **Reviewing** toolbar was not previously on the screen, it will now be displayed and the letters **TRK** appear in black on the status bar.*

⁕ If you wish to modify the marks Word uses to show the different types of modification, click the **Show** button on the **Reviewing** toolbar, click the **Options** option, make your changes then click **OK**.

⁕ Save the changes made to the document.

⁕ You must now make the document available to other users by copying it onto your network into one or more folders that the other users can access. Use the **File - Save As** command to do this, or copy the document using the **Windows Explorer**.

If you wish, you can give each copy of the document a different name.

📄 *To display a message to **Warn before printing, saving or sending a file that contains tracked changes or comments**, tick the appropriate option in the **Options** dialog box (**Tools - Options - Security** tab).*

> You can also activate the tracking of changes by double-clicking the **TRK** indicator on the status bar.

Merging documents

Merging involves bringing together in the original document all the changes (text insertion and deletion, formatting changes, etc.) and comments made by other users in the copies of that document. This is possible providing you activated tracking in the original document before making copies for the other users.

▪ Open the original document in which you wish to merge the changes and make sure you are in **Print Layout** view.

▪ For each copy of the document that is to be merged:

- use the **Tools - Compare and Merge Documents** command,

- select the folder containing the document that you wish to merge with the original and select the document within that folder,

- make sure that the **Legal blackline** option is not active. If this option is active, Word does not merge the documents but compares them and displays in a new document only what has changed between the original and the copy,

- open the list on the **Merge** tool button and click the **Merge into current document** option.

*The **Merge** option shows the result of the merge in the file selected in the **Compare and Merge Documents** dialog box: the **Merge into new document** option shows the result of the merge in a new document.*

A message may appear to tell you that the documents you are about to merge contain one or more conflicting formatting changes:

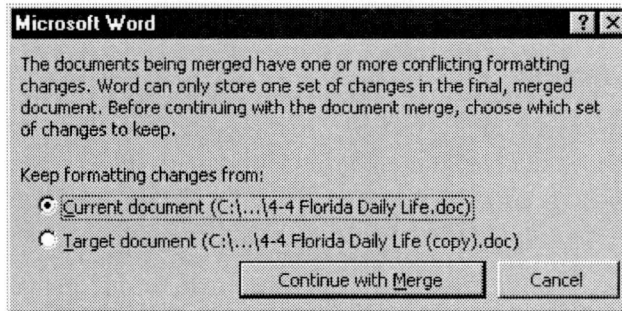

- if necessary, choose the document whose formatting changes you wish to keep, then click the **Continue with Merge** button.

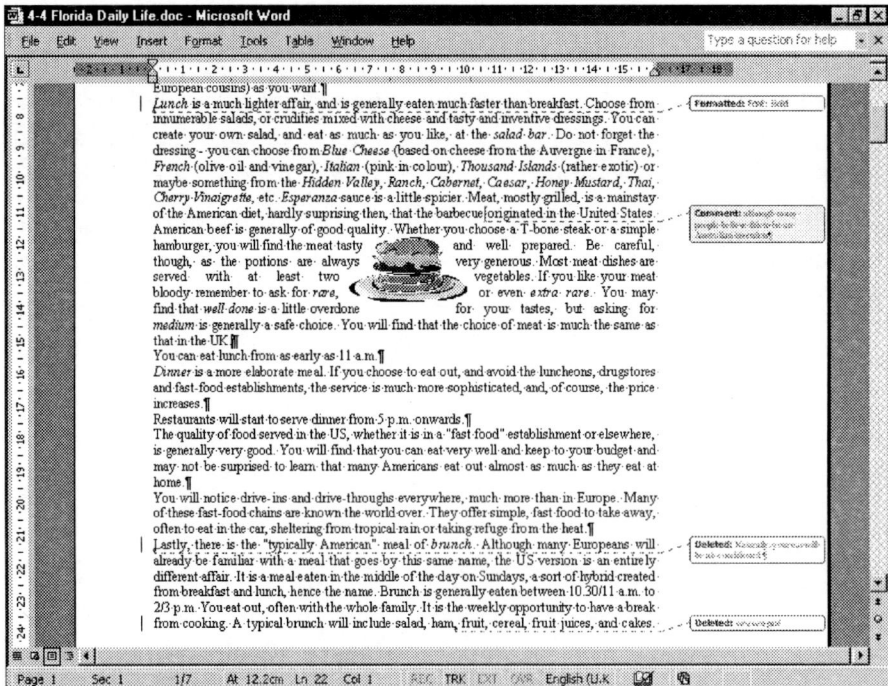

The changes and comments made by other users can now be seen in balloons; the changes and comments made by each user appear in a particular colour.
You may remember that if you want to see the name of the user who modified something or created a comment, simply move the mouse pointer over the corresponding balloon.

▪ Save the changes made to the document and close it.

Accepting or rejecting changes

You can either accept or reject the changes visible in the document after merging.

▪ Open the document in which the changes have been merged and position the pointer at the place where you wish to start reviewing the changes.

▪ Make sure you are in **Print Layout** view.

▪ If the balloons containing the changes are not visible in the document, show them with the **View - Markup** command.

▪ Make sure the **Reviewing** toolbar is visible.

▪ If you wish to review only the changes made by certain users, and not those made by all users, display the changes for the user(s) in question and hide all the others. To show a particular user's changes, click the **Show** button, point to the **Reviewers** option then tick the required user's name. Removing the tick before a user's name will hide the changes made by that user.

▪ If you wish to review the changes one by one, use the [⇥] or [⇥] tool button to move through the changes then click the [⬚▾] tool button to accept the change or [⬚▾] to reject it.

▪ To accept or refuse the changes from one or several users, show the changes made by the user(s) in question (if you have not already done so) then open the list on the [⬚▾] tool button and **Accept All Changes Shown** by clicking the appropriate option, or open the list on the [⬚▾] tool button and **Reject All Changes Shown**.

These two options will be unavailable if the changes made by all users are on display.

▪ To **Accept** or **Reject All Changes in Document**, open the list on the [⟳ ▾] tool button (to accept the changes) or the list on the [⟳ ▾] tool button (to reject the changes) and click the appropriate option.

▪ A message may appear, offering to start searching for changes from the top of the document: you can click the **Cancel** button, if you wish.

▪ Save the changes made to the document then close it.

📄 *You can use the options on the* [Final Showing Markup ▾] *tool to choose how Word should display the changes and comments. You can display the **Original** document, the **Original Showing Markup**, the **Final** document or the **Final Showing Markup**.*

2 ▪ Sending a file for review

*It is possible to send a copy of your document to one or more recipients so they can review it. This command is only available if you use the **Outlook 2002** e-mail application.*

Sending a document

▪ Open the document that you wish to send for review.

▪ **File - Send To - Mail Recipient (for Review)**

Please review '4-4 Florida Daily Life' - Message (HTML)

File Edit View Insert Format Tools Actions Help

Type a question for help

Send | Options... | Arial | 10

① Review

To...

Cc...

Subject: | Please review '4-4 Florida Daily Life'

Attach... | 4-4 Florida Daily Life.doc (129 KB)

Please review the attached document.

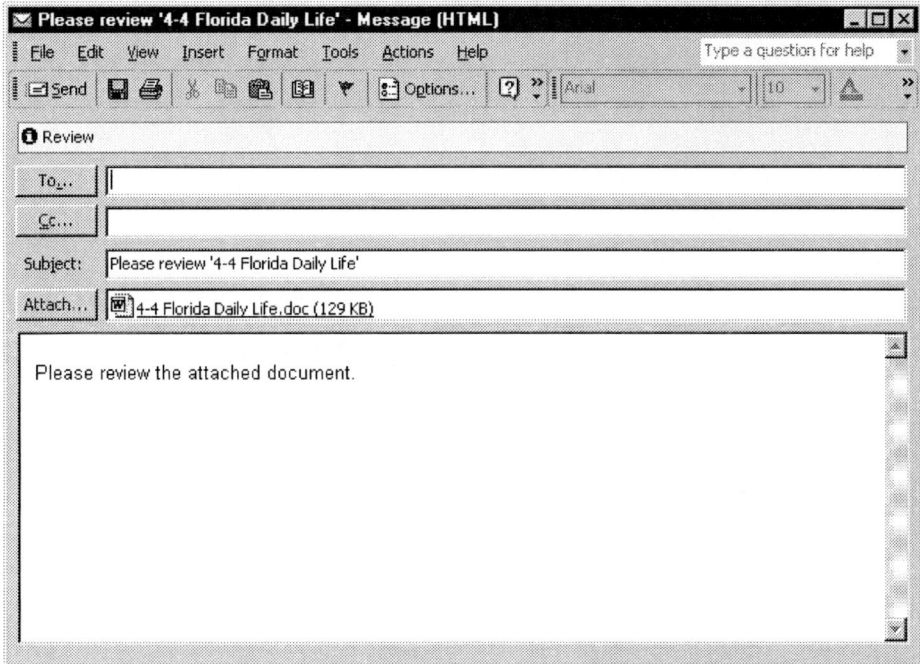

The Outlook 2002 new message window opens.

*The attached document is represented by an icon and appears in the main message pane of the window or in the **Attach** text box that lies below the **Subject** box.*

- In the **To** box, type the address(es) of the principal recipients of the message, separating each name with a semi-colon, or click the **To** button to select the address(es) in the address book.

- In the **Cc** (Carbon Copy) box, enter the address(es) of any recipients to whom you wish to send a carbon copy or click the **Cc** button to select from the address book.

A carbon copy of a message is sent for the recipient's information only and does not imply that you wish to receive a reply.

- If necessary, modify the text in the **Subject** box. By default, this box contains the text **Please review** followed by the name of the document.

* If you wish, add to or modify the text that appears in the main message pane of the window.

* Click the **Send** button.

Opening and reviewing a document

When you send a file for review, the recipient(s) must open the file from Outlook then review it in Word.

* On the **Outlook** bar of the **Outlook 2002** application, click the **Outlook Shortcuts** group then the **Inbox** folder.

* Double-click the message containing the document that is to be reviewed. Remember that the subject of the message is the text **Please review** followed by the document name.

* Double-click the file icon; this icon appears in the main message box or in the **Attachments** box beneath the **Subject** box.

Opening an attached file starts the application in which the document was created, wherever possible. It is, however, possible that you will see the following message:

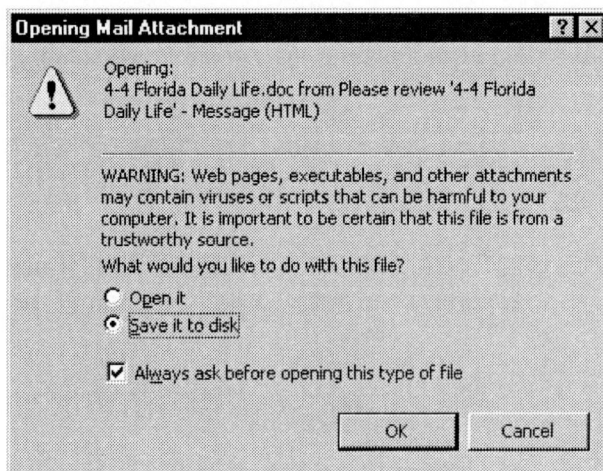

*The **Save it to disk** option saves the attached file on your hard disk and does not open it automatically. If you then wish to open the message from Outlook, you must double-click the attachment icon again and in the **Opening Mail Attachment** dialog box, open it using the **Open it** option.*

* Activate the **Open it** option.

* Deactivate the **Always ask before opening this type of file** option if you do not want this dialog box to appear again.

* Click **OK**.

  *Opening the file starts the Microsoft Word application. Tracking changes is active (the letters **TRK** will appear in black on the status bar) and the **Reviewing** toolbar displayed.*

* If necessary, go to **Print Layout** view (**View - Print Layout**) and make the necessary changes to the document.

* **File - Send To - Original Sender**

  *You can also click the **Reply with Changes** tool button on the **Reviewing** toolbar.*

  The message window reappears.

* If you wish, add any extra text to the main message body, in the lower half of the window.

* Click the **Send** button.

  The reviewed document appears on the screen.

* If you wish, save the changes made to the document (⊞) and/or save it under another name (**File - Save As**).

  The folder in which the document will be saved depends on the version of Windows. For Windows Me, the default folder is C:\WINDOWS\Temporary Internet Files\OLK70C4, for Windows 98, it is C:\WINDOWS\TEMP, for Windows 2000 Professional, the default folder is C:\Documents and settings\user name\Local Settings\Temporary Internet Files\OLK50 and for Windows NT, it is C:\Winnt\Profiles\Temporary Internet Files\Olk36.

*Depending on the version of Windows, you can also find a shortcut to the document in the **Recent** folder (Windows Me, Windows NT, Windows 2000 Professional) or in the **TEMP** folder (Windows 98). For Windows Me, the file path to the **Recent** folder is C:\WINDOWS\Application Data\Microsoft\Office, for Windows NT, it is C:\Winnt\Profiles\user name\Application Data\Microsoft\ Office, for Windows 2000 Professional, the file path is C:\Documents and settings\user name\Application Data\Microsoft\Office and for Windows 98, the file path to the **TEMP** folder is C:\WINDOWS.*

* Close the document and the Microsoft Word application using the **File - Exit** command.

* Close the message window, saving it. Click the ☒ button then click **Yes** on the message that asks if you want to save your changes.

  It is a good idea to save the message, so that the next time you open it, you will see the date when you replied.

Merging documents

When the message sender receives each message sent by the reviewers, he/she will open the attachment that corresponds to the document sent for review. A message will, at that time, ask if the changes should be merged into the original document.

* On the **Outlook** bar of the **Outlook 2002** application, click the **Outlook Shortcuts** group then the **Inbox** folder.

* Double-click the message containing the reviewed document. The subject of the message will be **RE: Please review** followed by the document name.

* Double-click the file icon. This icon appears in the main message body or in the **Attachments** box beneath the **Subject** box.

* Activate the **Open it** option.

* Click **OK**.

A message opens, offering to merge the changes made in the reviewed document into the original document.

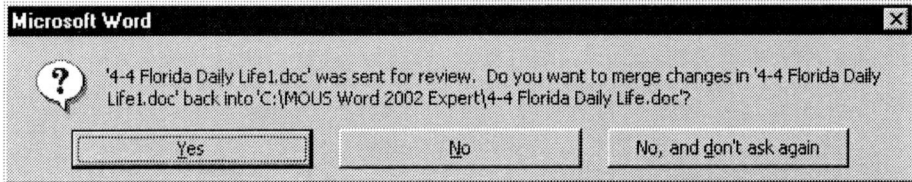

Microsoft Word ☒

(?) '4-4 Florida Daily Life1.doc' was sent for review. Do you want to merge changes in '4-4 Florida Daily Life1.doc' back into 'C:\MOUS Word 2002 Expert\4-4 Florida Daily Life.doc'?

[Yes]   [No]   [No, and don't ask again]

* Click **Yes**.

  To display the reviewed document, click No to stop the merge.

* Save the changes made to the original document then close it.

* Close the message window. Click the button corresponding to the message on the taskbar then click the ☒ button on the message window.

* If you sent the document for review to several other users, proceed in the same way for each document whose changes should be merged into the original document.

  📄 *If you click No on the message offering to merge the reviewed documents into the original document, you can always make the merge at a later time. To do this, make sure the reviewed document is active on the screen, use the Tools - Compare and Merge Documents command, select the original document, make sure the Legal blackline option is not active then click the Merge tool button.*

📖3 ▪ Protecting a document

Word will allow you to protect only certain elements of your document.

* Open the document concerned.

* **Tools - Protect Document**

OTHER ADVANCED FUNCTIONS
Lesson 4.4: Workgroups

* Click one of the options in the **Protect document for** frame:

Tracked changes The document's contents can be modified but any changes made are highlighted (as tracked changes) so they can be spotted easily. Tracking changes is activated and you cannot deactivate it. In addition, you can no longer accept or reject changes made to the document.

Comments The document's contents cannot be modified but you can insert comments.

Forms Users of a form can only access the form fields: modifications are prohibited in the rest of the document. When a form contains several sections, the **Sections** button can be used to choose which sections to protect.

* If required, give a password (of up to 15 characters) in the **Password (optional)** text box.

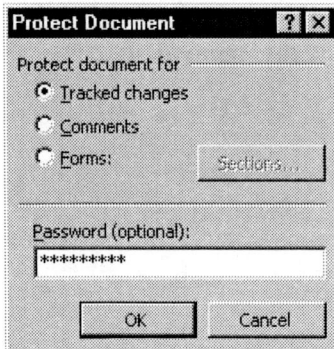

Asterisks replace the characters you type in. Be careful, as Word distinguishes between upper and lower case letters.

* Click **OK**.

For security reasons, Word will ask for the password again.

* Enter the password in the text box again and click **OK**.

*To remove the protection from a document, use the **Tools - Unprotect Document** command and, if requested, enter the **Password** in the text box and click **OK**.*

▦4 ▪ Associating a password with a document

The document can no longer be accessed without the password.

▪ Open the document concerned.

▪ **Tools - Options - Security** tab

▪ If you wish to control opening the document, enter a password in the **Password to open** text box.

▪ Tick the **Read-only recommended** option if you want Word to validate the password then prompt the user to open the document in read-only mode.

▪ If you wish to prevent unauthorised users from modifying or saving the document, enter a password in the **Password to modify** box. If the user does not know the password, he/she will only be able to open the document and read it.

File encryption options for this document		
Password to open:	********	Advanced...
File sharing options for this document		
Password to modify:		
☐ Read-only recommended		

You cannot see the password as you type it in, as it is replaced by asterisks on the screen. Be careful as Word differentiates between upper and lower case letters.

▪ Click **OK**.

▪ Type the password in the text box again to confirm it then click **OK**.

▪ Click the 🖫 tool button to save the password.

> 📄 *To remove a password associated with a document, delete the asterisks (*) from the corresponding text box in the dialog box (**Tools - Options - Security** tab).*

5 ▪ Creating several version of a document

A version is a "snapshot" that Word can take of your document, without creating a new file. The different versions are saved in the document, which saves disk space.

- ▪ Open the document concerned.

- ▪ **File - Versions**

- ▪ Click the **Save Now** button.

- ▪ Enter a comment.

- ▪ Click **OK**.

📄 *To create a version each time you close the document, activate the **Automatically save a version on close** option in the **Versions** dialog box (**File - Versions**).*

6 ▪ Managing versions of a document

Opening a version

- ▪ Open the document concerned.

- ▪ **File - Versions**

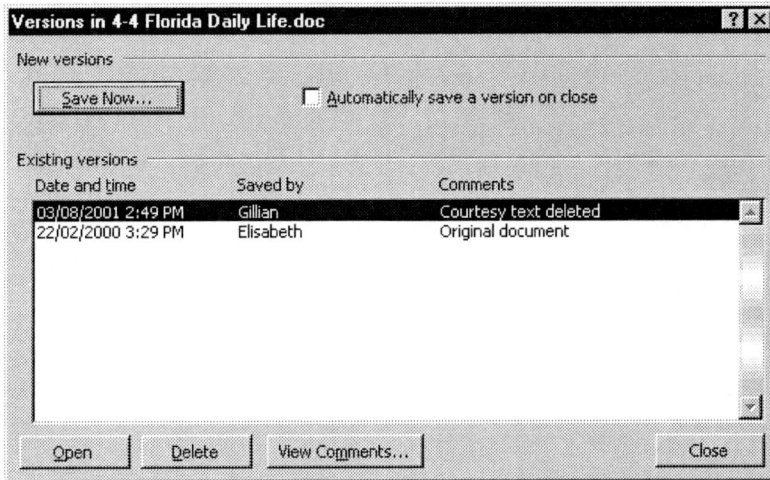

Versions in 4-4 Florida Daily Life.doc ? X

New versions

[Save Now...]   ☐ Automatically save a version on close

Existing versions

Date and time	Saved by	Comments
03/08/2001 2:49 PM	Gillian	Courtesy text deleted
22/02/2000 3:29 PM	Elisabeth	Original document

[Open]   [Delete]   [View Comments...]   [Close]

* Select the version you wish to consult.

* Click the **Open** button or simply double-click the version name.

> 📄 To save a version as a separate file, open it then use the **File - Save As** command.

Deleting a version

* Open the document concerned.

* **File - Versions**

* Select the version you wish to delete.

* Click the **Delete** button.

Confirm Version Delete X

(?) Are you sure you want to delete the selected version(s)? This action is not undoable.

[Yes]   [No]

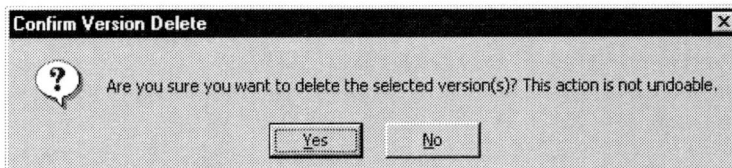

Word prompts you to confirm your deletion.

* Confirm by clicking the **Yes** button.

* Click the **Close** button.

Viewing a version's comments

* Open the document concerned.
* **File - Versions**
* Select the version whose comments you wish to see.
* Click the **View Comments** button.
* When you have finished reading the comments, click the **Close** button twice.

7 ▪ Defining the default group templates folder

By default, your custom templates (user templates) are saved in the Templates folder or in one of its subfolders. Depending on your version of Windows, this folder location can change: for Windows 98 and Me, the file path is C:\Windows\Application Data\Microsoft\Templates and for Windows 2000 Professional, the path is C:\Documents and settings\user name\Application Data\Microsoft\Templates. Only you can use these templates as they are saved on your hard disk (C:).
If you wish to create templates so other users can work with them (workgroup templates), you should save them on the network, in a folder that the other users can access, then define the default folder for the workgroup templates.

* **Tools - Options - File Locations** tab
* In the **File types** list, click the **Workgroup templates** option.

  *By default, there is no initial **Location** specified for **Workgroup templates**.*
* Click the **Modify** button.

  *A dialog box resembling the **Open** and **Save As** dialog boxes appears on the screen.*
* If the folder already exists, go to the network and double-click the folder concerned.

- If the folder does not exist, browse through the network until you find the place where you want to create the folder and click the ⌖ button. Enter the **Name** of the folder in the corresponding text box and click **OK**.

- Click **OK** to close the **Modify Location** dialog box.

Options	? ✕

View	General	Edit	Print	Save
Security		Spelling & Grammar		Track Changes
User Information		Compatibility		File Locations

File locations

File types: Location:

Documents	C:\My Documents
Clipart pictures	
User templates	C:\...\Microsoft\Templates
Workgroup templates	**\\Gwen\mousword2002**
AutoRecover files	C:\...\Application Data\Microsoft\Word
Tools	D:\...\MICROSOFT OFFICE\OFFICE10
Startup	C:\...\Microsoft\Word\STARTUP

Modify...

OK   Close

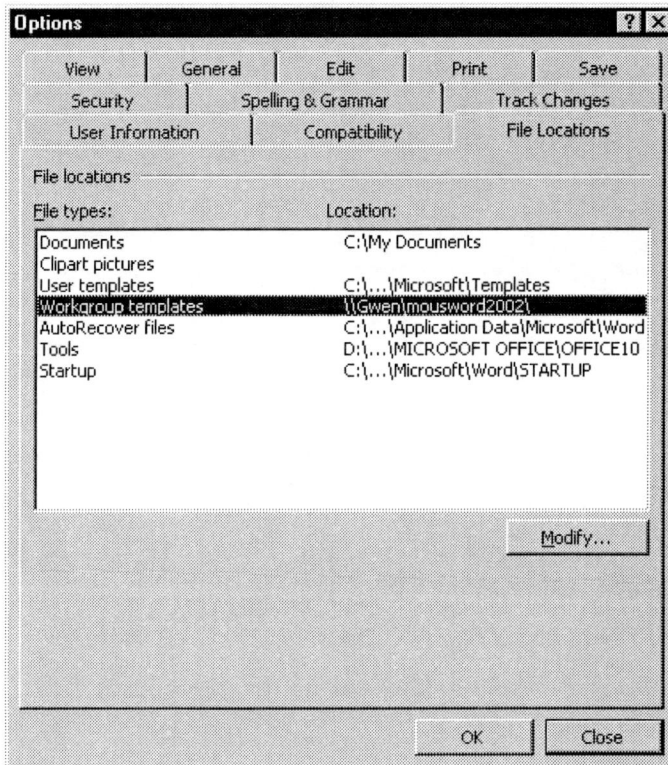

The file path to the folder now appears in the **Workgroup templates** *row.*

- Click **OK**.

📄 *When you save a template, the folder suggested by default in the **Save As** dialog box is the user templates folder. To save a template in the Workgroup templates folder, select this folder in the **Save in** list in the **Save As** dialog box.*

*Templates saved in the Workgroup templates folder can be seen on the **General** tab of the **Templates** dialog box (**File - New** then click the **General Templates** link in the task pane).*

🖫8 ▪ Using digital signatures

The **Microsoft Authenticode** technology used in Office XP allows you to use a digital certificate that will add a digital signature to files when you want to transmit them or make them available to other users. The certificate identifies you as the signer of the file and the signature confirms that since you signed it, the file has not been modified.

To obtain a digital certificate, you can apply for one through a commercial authority such as VeriSign or through your security administrator. You can also create your own digital certificate.

Creating your own digital certificate

When you create your own certificate, it will not be considered as authenticated.

▪ If it is not installed, install the **SelfCert.exe** file on your computer. Follow these instructions:

- Close all open programs.

- Insert the Microsoft Office XP CD-ROM into your drive and click the **SETUP.exe** icon in the **Office10** window. If this window does not open, go into the Windows **Control Panel** and double-click the **Add/Remove Programs** icon. In the list of programs installed, double-click the **Microsoft Office XP** option.

- Make sure the **Add or Remove Features - Change which features are installed or remove specific features** option is active then click the **Next** button.

- Click the plus sign (+) associated with the **Office Shared Features**.

- Click the black down arrow on the icon for **Digital Signature for VBA Projects** and choose the **Run from My Computer** option.

- Click the **Update** button.

- Click **OK** on the message that informs you that your Microsoft Office installation has been updated successfully.

- Click **OK** on the **Add/Remove Programs Properties** dialog box then close the **Control Panel** window or close the **Office 10** window.

▪ Open the **Windows Explorer** and double-click the **Selfcert.exe** file, which is generally located in the **C:\Program Files\Microsoft Office\Office10** folder.

▪ Enter **Your name** in the corresponding text box.

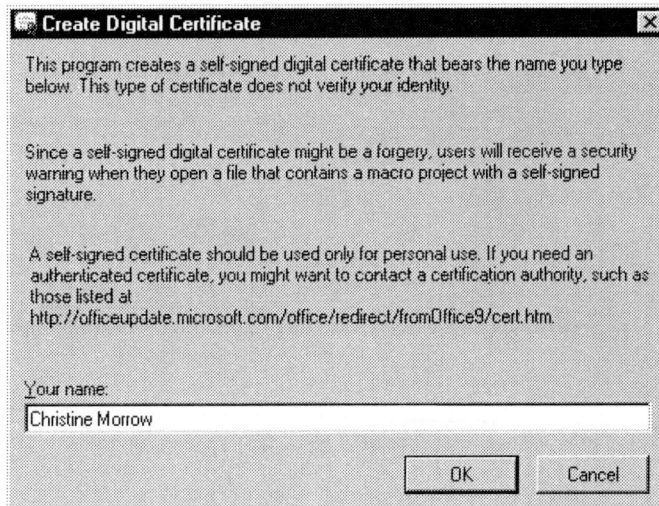

▪ Click **OK**.

* Click **OK** on the message that tells you the new certificate has been created successfully.

* Close the Windows Explorer window by clicking its ☒ button.

* Open the Microsoft Word 2002 application again.

Adding a signature to a file

* Open the file to which you want to add the digital signature.

* **Tools - Options**

* Click the **Security** tab then the **Digital Signatures** button.

* Click the **Add** button.

* If necessary, validate any messages that may appear on the screen by clicking the **Yes** button.

  These messages tell you of problems which may occur subsequently; if you click ***No***, *you can fix any potential problems before adding a digital signature to the document.*

* Select the certificate you want to use.

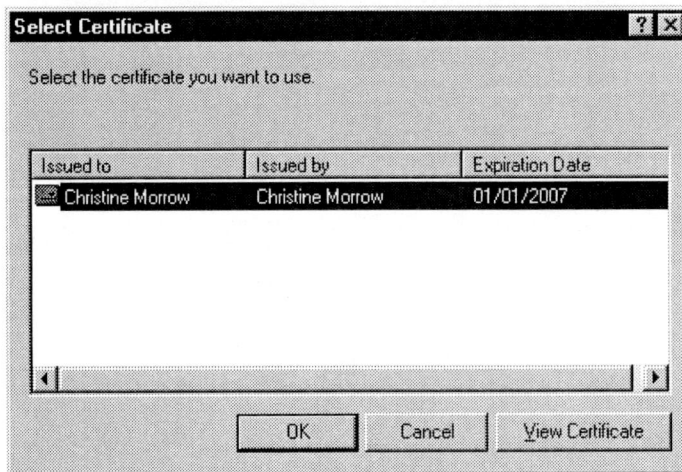

▪ Click **OK**.

In the **Digital Signature** dialog box, you can now see the signer's name corresponding to the previously selected certificate.

▪ If you activate the **Attach certificates with newly added signatures** option, users of the digitally signed file will be able to open the certificate to obtain further details.

▪ Click the **OK** button twice.

The term *[Signed]* now appears next to the document name on the title bar and this icon: can be seen on the status bar.

If you try to save any subsequent modifications to the document, a message will appear to inform you that these changes will remove the signature from the file:

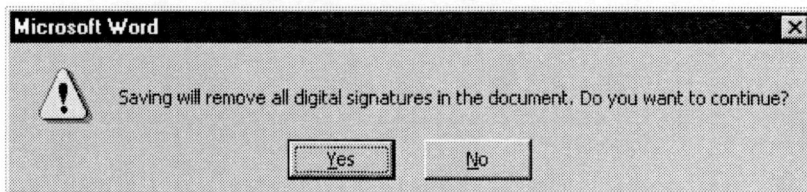

Microsoft Word ❌

⚠ Saving will remove all digital signatures in the document. Do you want to continue?

Yes   No

📄 *If the user of a digitally signed document wishes to know who has signed it, he/she can open the **Digital Signature** dialog box by double-clicking the 🔖 icon on the status bar.*

*To show the digital certificate and learn more about the signer, the user should click the **View Certificate** button on the **Digital Signature** dialog box (which is opened by double-clicking the 🔖 icon). As a user-created certificate is unauthenticated, a message will appear under the **General** tab to inform the reader that the certificate is not trusted. To enable trust on that certificate, you can click the **Install Certificate** button to add the certificate to the Trusted Root Certification Authorities store (the area of your system where certificates and lists of issued and revoked certificates are stored).*

Removing a digital signature

※ Open the file from which you wish to remove the digital signature.

※ Use the **Tools - Options** command, click the **Security** tab then the **Digital Signatures** button or double-click the 🔖 icon on the status bar.

※ Select the signature you wish to delete then click the **Remove** button.

※ Click **OK** twice.

Below, you can see **Practice Exercise** 4.4. This exercise is made up of 8 steps. If you do not know how to do one of the steps, go back to the title that corresponds to that particular lesson. When you have finished, you can check your work by reading the **Solution** that follows.

All the parts of this exercise are likely to be tested on the MOUS exam.

☞ Practice Exercise 4.4

*To work on practice exercise 4.4, open the **4-4 Florida Daily Life.doc** document, located in the **MOUS Word 2002 Expert** folder.*

1. If necessary, activate tracking changes then merge the active document (**4-4 Florida Daily Life.doc**) with the **4-4 Florida Daily Life (copy).doc** document which is in the **MOUS Word 2002 Expert**; this document contains the same text as the **4-4 Florida Daily Life.doc** document but certain changes have been made to it. Accept all the changes made except the deletion of the text **or even paté** and the application of italics to the word **seafood**.

   To continue the rest of this exercise, you will need to use two computers.

2. From the first computer, send the **4-4 Florida Daily Life.doc** document (this is the active document) for review to another user (in this case, use the e-mail address of the second computer you are using). Do not modify the text in the **Subject** box or the text of the message.
   Using the second computer, open the e-mail message you sent from the first computer. Review the **4-4 Florida Daily Life.doc** document attached to this message, following the instructions below, then send the message back to its sender (using the e-mail address of the other computer you are using):
   - apply a font size of **13** and underline the words **Breakfast** and **Lunch** visible on page 1.
   - apply a **green** font colour to the main title of the document (**DAILY LIFE IN FLORIDA**).

Save the changes made to the document then close it and the Microsoft Word application. Close the message window, saving the message.

Return to the first computer and open the message containing the reviewed document then merge the changes made to the reviewed document into the original (C:\MOUS Word 2002 Expert\4-4 Florida Daily Life.doc).
Finish by saving the changes made to the original 4-4 Florida Daily Life.doc document then closing the message window.

3. Protect the changes made to the **4-4 Florida Daily Life.doc**; use the password **flochange** (in lowercase letters).

4. Set the password **dailyflo** which will be required before the **4-4 Florida Daily Life.doc** document can be.

5. Delete the **COURTESY** heading (page 5) and the associated text (up to **as soon as you are introduced**). Create a version of the document with the associated comment **Courtesy text deleted**.

6. Open the first version of the document; the comment for this version is **Original document**. Close this version then maximise the **4-4 Florida Daily Life.doc** document window.

7. Define the default workgroup templates folder. If necessary, create this folder. Choose any name and location on the network you wish.
Save the changes made to the document.

8. If necessary, install the **SelfCert.exe** file on your computer then create your own digital certificate, identified by your own first name and surname. Add this digital signature to the **4-4 Florida Daily Life.doc** document then close it.

If you would like to practise these features more, on another document, you should work through Summary Exercise 4, on OTHER ADVANCED FUNCTIONS. You will find the summary exercises at the end of the book.

It is often possible to perform a task in several different ways, but here, only the easiest solution is presented. You can go back to the corresponding lesson if you want to see other techniques you could use.

Solution to Exercise 4.4

1. To activate tracking changes, use the **Tools - Track Changes** command (the letters **TRK** are displayed in black on the status bar).

   To merge the active document (4-4 Florida Daily Life.doc) with the 4-4 Florida Daily Life (copy).doc document, use the **Tools - Compare and Merge Documents** command.
   If necessary, select the **MOUS Word 2002 Expert** folder then the **4-4 Florida Daily Life (copy).doc** document. Make sure the **Legal blackline** option is inactive, open the list on the **Merge** button then click the **Merge into current document** option.

   To accept all the changes except the deletion of the text "or even paté" and the application of italics to the word "seafood", make sure you are in **Print Layout** view. If they are not visible, display the markup balloons that show what changes have been made, with the **View - Markup** command, and make sure the **Reviewing** toolbar is on display (**View - Toolbars - Reviewing**). Press the Ctrl Home keys to place the insertion point at the top of the document.

   Click the tool button then click the tool button; click the tool button twice and then click the tool button; click the tool button then the tool button (to reject the text deletion). Click twice then (to reject the italic formatting); next, click the tool button one last time. Click the **Cancel** button to finish.

2. To send the 4-4 Florida Daily Life.doc document from your computer to another user (the e-mail address of your second computer) for review, use the **File - Send To - Mail Recipient (for Review)** command. Click the **To** text box, enter the recipient's address then click the **Send** button.

To open the message you sent from the first computer, work on the second computer and in the **Outlook 2002** application window, click the **Outlook Shortcuts** group then the **Inbox**. Double-click the message whose subject is **Please review '4-4 Florida Daily Life.doc'**. double-click the icon corresponding to the 4-4 Florida Daily Life file to open it, activate the **Open it** option and click **OK**.

To review the 4-4 Florida Daily Life document as described in step 2, make sure you are in **Print Layout** view (**View - Print Layout**), select the word **Breakfast** then hold down the Ctrl key and select the word **Lunch**. Click the **Font Size** list 12 on the **Formatting** toolbar, type **13**, press the key then click the U tool button. Next, select the **DAILY LIFE IN FLORIDA** heading, open the list on the A tool button and choose the colour called **Green**. Send the document back to its sender by clicking the **Reply with Changes** button then click the **Send** button on the message window.

To save the changes made to the document, click the tool button.

To close the document as well as the Microsoft Word application, activate the **File - Exit** command.

To close the message window, saving the message, click the X button then the **Yes** button on the message that asks if you want to save your changes.

To merge the changes made to the reviewed document back in the original document (C:\MOUS Word 2002 Expert\4-Florida Daily Life.doc), return to the first computer. In **Outlook 2002**, if necessary, click the **Outlook Shortcuts** group then the **Inbox**. Double-click the message called **RE: Please review '4-4 Florida Daily Life.doc'**. Double-click the icon of the 4-4 Florida Daily Life.doc file then click the **Open it** option and

OK. Click **Yes** on the message that asks if you want to merge the reviewed document with the original 4-4 Florida Daily Life.doc document.

To save the changes made to the original 4-4 Florida Daily Life.doc document, click the 🖫 tool button.

To close the message window, activate it by clicking the corresponding button on the taskbar then click ☒ at the top of the window.

3. To protect the changes made to the **4-4 Florida Daily Life.doc** document, use the **Tools - Protect Document** command then leave the **Tracked changes** option active.

Enter **flochange** (in lowercase) in the **Password (optional)** text box and click **OK**.

Enter the password again in the **Reenter password to open** text box and click **OK**.

4. To associate the "dailyflo" password with opening the **4-4 Florida Daily Life.doc** document, use the **Tools - Options** command then click the **Security** tab.

Enter **dailyflo** (in lowercase letters) in the **Password to open** text box then click **OK**.

Enter the password again in the **Reenter password to open** box and click **OK**.

Save the document by clicking the 🖫 tool button.

5. To delete the "COURTESY" heading on page 5, and its associated text, select this heading and text and press the ⌈Del⌋ key.

To create a version of this document, use the **File - Versions** command. Click the **Save Now** button, type **Courtesy text deleted** in the **Comments on version** text box and click **OK**.

6. To open the first version of the document, use the **File - Versions** command and double-click the version called **Original document**.

To close the window of this version, click the ☒ button at the top of the document window containing that version (check this on the title bar, the term **Version** appears).

To maximise the **4-4 Florida Daily Life.doc** window, click the ▢ button at the top right of the document window.

7. To define the default folder for saving workgroup templates, activate the **Tools - Options** command and click the **File Locations** tab.
In the **File types** list, click the **Workgroup templates** option and click the **Modify** button.
Go on to your network, choose the folder required or create it if it does not exist yet and click **OK**.
Click **OK** to close the **Options** dialog box.

To save the changes made to the document, click the ▣ tool button on the **Standard** toolbar.

8. If the SelfCert.exe file is not installed on your computer, close all the open applications, put the Microsoft Office XP CD-ROM in your drive and click the **SETUP.EXE** icon in the **Office10** window.
Make sure the **Add or Remove Features - Change which features are installed or remove specific features** option is active then click the **Next** button.

Click the plus sign (+) associated with the **Office Shared Features**.
Click the black down arrow on the icon for **Digital Signature for VBA Projects** and choose the **Run from My Computer** option.
Click the **Update** button then **OK** on the message that informs you that your Microsoft Office installation has been updated successfully.
Close the **Office10** window by clicking its ☒ button.

To create your own digital certificate using your name and surname, open the **Windows Explorer** and double-click the **Selfcert.exe** file, generally located in the **C:\Program Files\Microsoft Office\Office10** folder.

Type your own first name and surname in the **Your name** text box and click **OK**.

Click **OK** on the message that tells you the new certificate has been created successfully then close the Windows Explorer window by clicking its ⊠ button. Open the Microsoft Word 2002 application again then open the **4-4 Florida Daily Life.doc** document, located in the **MOUS Word 2002 Expert** folder.

To add your digital signature to the 4-4 Florida Daily Life.doc document, use the **Tools - Options** command, click the **Security** tab then the **Digital Signatures** button.

Click the **Add** button then click **Yes** on any warning messages that appear.

Select the certificate you want to use and click **OK** three times.

To close the 4-4 Florida Daily Life.doc document, use the **File - Close** command.

OTHER ADVANCED FUNCTIONS
Lesson 4.5: Web pages

OTHER ADVANCED FUNCTIONS
Lesson 4.5: Web pages

1 ▪ Saving a document as a Web page

By saving a document as a Web page, you can subsequently publish it on an Internet or intranet site.

▪ Open the document you want to use to create the Web page.

▪ **File - Save as Web Page**

▪ If necessary, in the **File name** box, type a new name or modify the current name of the document.

▪ Click the **Change Title** button if you want to change the page heading.

This page heading is displayed on the title bar of the Web browser.

▪ Select the folder in which to save the document.

▪ Click the **Save** button.

A confirmation window may appear if the browser does not support some of the document functions.

By default, when a Web page is composed of elements, such as bullets or background pictures, Word groups these elements into a folder called a supporting files folder. This folder's name is the name of the Web page, followed by __files__. It is created in the folder containing the Web page. If you need to move or copy the Web page, you must also move this folder to preserve its links with the Web page.

To publish a Web page so that it can be viewed on a network (the Internet or an intranet), open Windows Explorer, select the Web page (.htm file) and its folder of supporting files (a folder with the same name as the .htm file plus __files__), if it has one, and copy them onto a Web server.

⊞2 ▪ Opening Web pages in Microsoft Word

▪ **File - Open** or ▣

▪ Open the **Files of type** list and choose the **Web Pages and Web Archives (*.htm; *.html; *.mht; *.mhtml)** option.

▪ Go to the folder in which the Web page (.htm file) concerned is stored by double-clicking that folder's icon.

▪ Double-click the Web page you want to open, or select it and click the **Open** button.

⊞3 ▪ Modifying a Web page

▪ Open the Web page you want to modify, using the **File - Open** command.

▪ Modify the Web page like a normal Word document, using the standard tools and commands.

▪ **File - Save** or ▣ or ⌨ Ctrl **S**

▪ Close the Web page by clicking the ⊠ button.

> 📄 *To update a Web page on a Web server, make a new copy of the revised .htm file (and its supporting files, if there are any) and replace the old version of the file on the server.*
>
> *To delete a Web page (.htm file) and any supporting files from your hard disk, use the **File - Open** command. Select the folder containing the Web page you want to delete then the .htm file. Press the ⌨ Del key and confirm the deletion by clicking **Yes**. When a Web page is deleted, the folder of supporting files is deleted automatically. To finish, click the ⊠ button on the **Open** dialog box.*

📄 *To delete a Web page and its supporting files from a Web server, use the Windows Explorer to access the server and (if appropriate) the folder containing the Web page. Select the Web file (.htm) and press the* Del *key.*

Deleting items from your hard disk does not affect the items on the Web server and vice versa.

4 ▪ Previewing a Web Page

▪ Use Word's **File - Open** command to open the Web page (.htm file) you want to view in a browser.

▪ **File - Web Page Preview**

The Web page opens in the default browser and you see it as it would appear on the Internet or an intranet site.

▪ Once you have seen the page, close the browser.

▪ Close the Web page (.htm file) in the same way as you would close any document.

5 ▪ Inserting a hyperlink

▪ Open the file in which you wish to insert the link.

▪ Place the insertion point where you wish to insert the link or select the text which you are going to use as a link.

▪ **Insert - Hyperlink** or 🖼 or Ctrl **K**

▪ Click the **Existing File or Web Page** shortcut on the **Link to** bar.

*The **Create New Document** shortcut allows you to create a link to a document that does not already exist.*

▪ In the **Text to display** box, enter or edit the text that is going to appear as the hyperlink.

▪ Fill in the **Address** box using one of the following techniques:

- In the **Address** box, type the name and full path of the file or the URL of the Web page to which the link leads.

- Click the **Current Folder** shortcut, select the drive (using the **Look in** list) and folder in which the target file is stored then select the file in question. You can choose to target a folder, in which case, when the link is clicked, the folder will open in Windows Explorer.

- Click the **Browsed Pages** shortcut and select the link's target page from a list of recently viewed Web pages.

- Click the **Recent Files** shortcut to see a list of recently used files and choose the link's target file from among them.

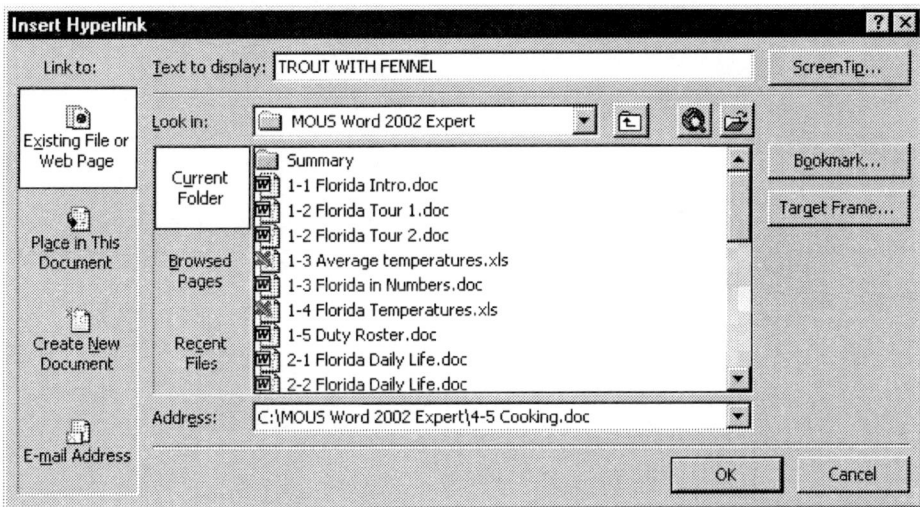

▪ To change the text that appears in the link's screen tip, click the **ScreenTip** button, type your text then click **OK**. By default, the screen tip contains the address of the target.

▪ The **Bookmark** button lets you select the named location in the document that is to be targeted by the link, if appropriate.

▪ Click **OK**.

The hyperlink appears in blue. If you have not selected or specified a text, the link appears as the document's path. When you point to the link (without clicking), a screen tip appears, which is by default the file or Web page's address.

▪ To activate the hyperlink, hold down the `Ctrl` key and click the link.

The document or Web page appears on the screen.

📄 *You can create as many hyperlinks as you like in a document; the links can go to all sorts of documents, including Word and Excel documents, Web pages and so on.*

Below, you can see **Practice Exercise** 4.5. This exercise is made up of 5 steps. If you do not know how to do one of the steps, go back to the title that corresponds to that particular lesson. When you have finished, you can check your work by reading the **Solution** that follows.

Steps in the exercise that are likely to be tested on the exam are preceded by this symbol: ▦. However, it is a good idea to complete all the steps in the exercise, to ensure that you have understood all the points discussed in the lesson.

☞ Practice Exercise 4.5

*To work on practice exercise 4.5, open the **4-5 Trout Recipe.doc** document located in the **MOUS Word 2002 Expert** folder.*

▦ 1. Create a Web page from the **4-5 Trout Recipe.doc** document and save the Web page in the **MOUS Word 2002 Expert** folder. You do not need to modify the document name but add a **Microwave Cooking** title to the page. Close the Web page.

▦ 2. Open the **4-5 Trout Recipe.htm** Web page that is in the **MOUS Word 2002 Expert** folder.

▦ 3. Change the first item in the list of ingredients that appears on the **4-5 Trout Recipe.htm** Web page (this should be your active file). This first item should read:
2 trout fillets weighing 250g (½ lb) each

4. Preview the **4-5 Trout Recipe.htm** Web page (this is the active file) then close your browser.

5. From the **TROUT WITH FENNEL** title in the **4-5 Trout Recipe.htm** Web page, create a hyperlink to the **4-5 Cooking.doc** document which is in the **MOUS Word 2002 Expert** folder. Activate the hyperlink to go to the **4-5 Cooking.doc** document then close the **4-5 Cooking.doc** document.

Finish by saving the changes made to the **4-5 Trout Recipe.htm** document then close it.

If you would like to practise these features more, on another document, you should work through Summary Exercise 4, on OTHER ADVANCED FUNCTIONS. You will find the summary exercises at the end of the book.

It is often possible to perform a task in several different ways, but here, only the easiest solution is presented. You can go back to the corresponding lesson if you want to see other techniques you could use.

Solution to Exercise 4.5

1. To create a Web page from the 4-5 Trout Recipe.doc document, use the **File - Save as Web Page** command. If necessary, select the **MOUS Word 2002 Expert** folder. Click the **Change Title** button and type **Microwave Cooking** in the **Page title** text box then click **OK**. Click the **Save** button then click **Continue** on the message that describes which features are not supported by the browser.
   To close the Web page, use the **File - Close** command.

2. To open the 4-5 Trout Recipe.htm Web page, which is in the MOUS Word 2002 Expert folder, activate the **File - Open** command then if necessary, select the **MOUS Word 2002 Expert** folder.
   Open the **Files of type** list and select the **Web Pages and Web Archives (*.htm;*.html;*.mht;*.mhtml)** option.
   Double-click the **4-5 Trout Recipe.htm** file.

3. To change the first item in the list of ingredients that appears on the 4-5 Trout Recipe.htm Web page as shown in step 3, select the text **450g (1lb) trout fillets** and press the ⎡Del⎦ key. Type the text **2 trout fillets weighing 250g (½ lb) each**.

   Save the changes made to the Web page by clicking the 🖫 tool button on the **Standard** toolbar.

4. To preview the 4-5 Trout Recipe.htm Web page, activate the **File - Web Page Preview** command.
   To close the browser, click the ☒ button on its window.

5. To create a hyperlink to the 4-5 Cooking.doc document (in the MOUS Word 2002 Expert folder) from the "TROUT WITH FENNEL" title in the 4-5 Trout Recipe.doc Web page, select the **TROUT WITH FENNEL** title at the top of the 4-5 Trout Recipe.htm Web page and click the [icon] tool button.

Click the **Address** text box, type **C:\MOUS Word 2002 Expert\4-5 Cooking.doc** (or if you prefer, select the folder and file using the **Look in** drop-down list) then click **OK**.

To activate the hyperlink you just created, and go to the 4-5 Cooking.doc document, hold down the [Ctrl] key and click the **TROUT WITH FENNEL** hyperlink.
To close the 4-5 Cooking.doc document, use the **File - Close** command.

To save the changes made to the 4-5 Trout Recipe.htm Web page, click the [icon] tool button.

To close the 4-5 Trout Recipe.htm Web page, use **File - Close**.

SUMMARY EXERCISES

Summary Exercise 1 — DOCUMENT CONTENTS AND PRESENTATION

Open the **Summary 1.doc** document in the **Summary** folder, which is in the **MOUS Word 2002 Expert**.

Insert a page break in the empty paragraph above the text **Audience numbers for February** (page 2).

Sort the list concerning the first screening dates: sort the list in ascending order by the date then by film name.

Create a character style based on the presentation of the text **THE THIRD MAN** and call this style **Film Title**. Create a paragraph style based on the presentation of the **First screenings** paragraph and call this style **Screening**.
Apply the **Film title** style to the **THE ITALIAN JOB** and **THE COMMITMENTS** titles.
Apply the **Screening** style to the **Audience numbers for January** and **Audience numbers for February** titles.

Delete the style called **TP**.

In the table on page 2 of the document, calculate the total number of entries for each week.

Underneath the **Audience numbers for February** heading, insert the **February** worksheet from the **Films.xls** workbook, which is in the **Summary** folder within the **MOUS Word 2002 Expert**.

Under this table, make a chart by importing data from the **February** worksheet from the **Films.xls** workbook which is in the **Summary** folder (within the **MOUS Word 2002 Expert** folder). This chart will represent the entries from the four weekly screenings from February. You should obtain the chart shown below:

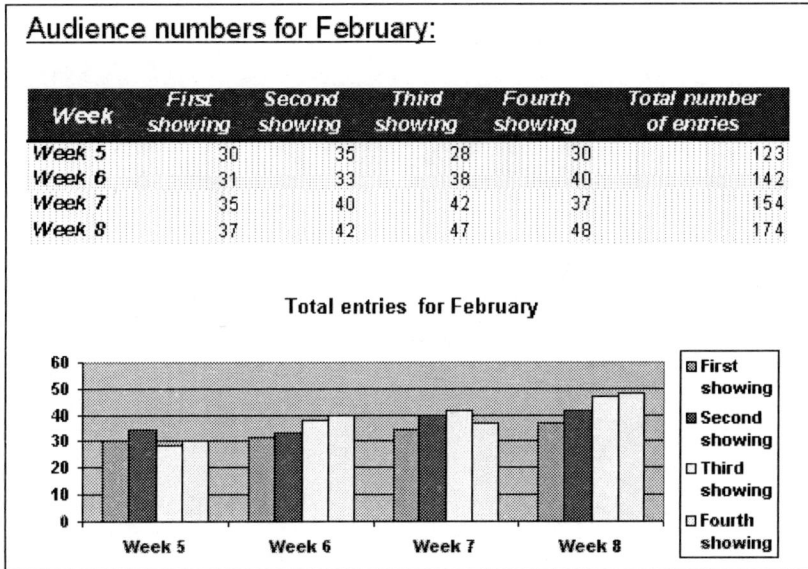

Audience numbers for February:

Week	First showing	Second showing	Third showing	Fourth showing	Total number of entries
Week 5	30	35	28	30	123
Week 6	31	33	38	40	142
Week 7	35	40	42	37	154
Week 8	37	42	47	48	174

Total entries for February

To obtain this result, you will have to invert the data series, delete the last column (called **Total number of entries**) from the datasheet, change the chart type, add the **Total entries for February** title to the chart then resize the chart to make it bigger.

Insert the drawing object shown on the illustration below into the second paragraph that follows the **NEXT MONTH** heading on page 4, following the instructions below:

- The object should be inserted in a drawing canvas: you must reduce the size of this canvas.

- The object is made with the AutoShape called **Up Ribbon** in the **Stars and Banners** category.

- Apply a **Sea Green** colour to the object's background and apply **Teal** as the outline colour.

- Apply a **Comic sans MS** font in size **20** to the text **THE ADVENTURES OF ROBIN HOOD** then centre the text.

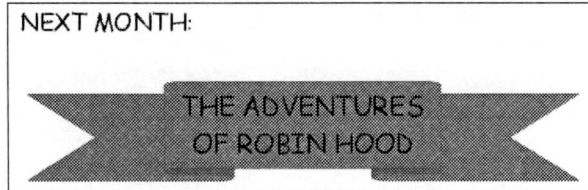

NEXT MONTH:

THE ADVENTURES
OF ROBIN HOOD

Under the paragraph **Directed by Michael Curtiz**, insert the picture called **Robin.tif** which is in the **Summary** folder. Change its wrapping style, its size and its position to obtain this presentation:

THE ADVENTURES
OF ROBIN HOOD

directed by Michael Curtiz - 1938

The times are sad in England. The good king Richard, much loved by his subjects, has left to fight in the Crusades. During his absence, the dastardly Prince John has taken the crown. The people are oppressed by this tyrant. Their only hope is Robin Hood, the bandit with a big heart, defender of the poor, and upholder of justice. Pursued by the Sheriff of Nottingham, Robin finds refuge in the forest of Sherwood with his allies Little John and Friar Tuck....

The solution to this exercise is called **Solution 1.doc**.

Open the **Summary 2.doc** document located in the **Summary** folder within the **MOUS Word 2002 Expert** folder.

Go to the place in the document that is marked by the **Henry VIII** bookmark. Delete this bookmark.

At the end of the paragraph about the **Cleveland Bay**, insert the footnote: **This breed is very popular as a police horse in many countries**.
Change the appearance of the footnotes so that they are numbered 1, 2, 3... and not lettered a, b, c...

Make an outline of the document using its custom styles. To do this, apply an outline level 1 to the **MAIN HEADING** style, level 2 to **PRIMARY HEADING** and level 3 to **SUBHEADING**.

At the beginning of the document, under the **TABLE OF CONTENTS** paragraph, insert the table of contents. You should apply a **Distinctive** format and the table should have three levels of headings.

Complete the index entries by creating an index entry after the text **The true origins of the Shire**: the main entry is **Draught horse**, the subentry **Shire**.

At the end of the document, under the paragraph **INDEX**, insert the index, using the **Modern** style.

The solution to this exercise is called **Solution 2A.doc**.

Create a master document and insert the subdocuments **Summary 2-1.doc** and **Summary 2-2.doc** from the **Summary** folder in the **MOUS Word 2002 Expert** folder.
Save this master document as **Cumbria.doc** in the **Summary** folder in the **MOUS Word 2002 Expert** folder. Close this document then open it again.

Go to **Print Layout** view and type the text **Cumbria** on the first page, above the section break. Format this text as you please.

Return to **Outline** view and, if necessary, collapse the subdocuments so that you can delete the last paragraph of the document (which is empty).

Expand the master document then number the headings using the **1**, **1.1**, **1.1.1** format.

Print the outline of the master document then print the entire master document.

The solution to this exercise is called **Solution 2B.doc**.

Summary Exercise 3   MAIL MERGE

Create the form illustrated below:

```
┌──────────────────────────────────────────────────────────┐
│  ┌────────────────────────────────────────────────────┐  │
│  │ INFORMATION ABOUT ACCOMMODATION TO RENT            │  │
│  └────────────────────────────────────────────────────┘  │
│                                                           │
│   Type:                  [One-room ▾]                     │
│   Surface area:          [      ] sq ft.                  │
│   Monthly rent:          [      ]                         │
│                                                           │
│   Conditions: ──────────────────────────────────────     │
│                                                           │
│   Public transport close by:   ☐                          │
│   Amenities close by:          ☐                          │
│   Animals permitted:           ☒                          │
│                                                           │
│   Particular requirements:    [      ]                    │
│                                                           │
└──────────────────────────────────────────────────────────┘
```

The items to be included in the drop-down list are: **One-room, One-bed, Two-bed, Bungalow, Semi** and **Detached**.
The text field for the surface area is of **Number** type.

The monthly rent is a **Number** field with a currency format.

The check box relating to **Animals permitted** should be checked by default.

The solution to this exercise is called **Solution 3.dot** and can be found in the **MOUS Templates** folder.

SUMMARY EXERCISES

Open the **Summary 3-1.doc** document in the **Summary** folder in the **MOUS Word 2002** folder. Create a mail merge with this document as the main document and the **Summary 3-2.doc** document as the data source file. You should insert the fields into the **Summary 3-1** main document as shown below:

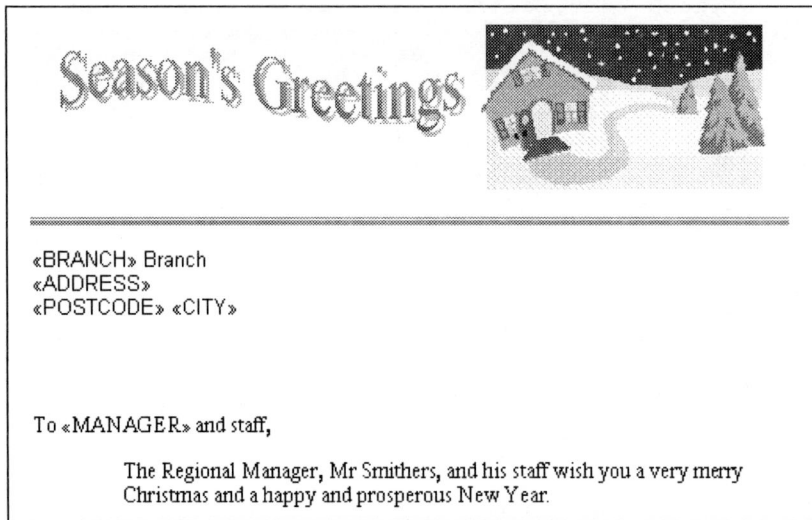

Run the mail merge in a new document, check the result of the merge by looking at the first three letters then close the document without saving it.

Make the following changes to the **Summary 3-2.doc** data list, using the data entry grid:

- The BRAID HILL branch has moved. The address has changed from "3 Memorial Drive" to **7 Main Street**.

- A new branch has opened. Its details are: **MARKET ST**, **Miss Adams**, **2 Market Street**, **FERN GROVE**, **4120**. Create a record for this branch.

- The BLACKFORD branch in Herston has been closed. Delete the corresponding record.

The solution to the main document is called **Solution 3A.doc** and the solution to the data file is called **Solution 3B.doc**.

Summary Exercise 4   OTHER ADVANCED FUNCTIONS

Open the **Summary 4.doc** document in the **Summary** folder in the **MOUS Word 2002 Expert** folder.

Create a macro that will set two left aligned tab stops at 5 cm and 12 cm, with a tab leader, in the paragraphs that give the dates and times of film screenings. Call this macro **Tabs** and save it in the active document (**Summary 4.doc**).
A toolbar has been created especially for this document, called **Summary 4 Formatting** and is saved in the **Summary 4.doc** document. Add a tool button to this toolbar that will run the **Tabs** macro. The tool button should have the text **Tabs** on it.

Run this macro on the paragraphs that show the date and times of film screenings for April and May.

Delete the tool button (open document) from the **Summary 4 Formatting** toolbar.

Create a version of the document with the comment **Intermediate version**. Delete the version called **First version**.

Use the password **MOUS** (in uppercase) to protect the active document from changes.

The solution to this exercise is called **Solution 4.doc** (use the password MOUS).

MICROSOFT Word 2002 Expert				
Table of objectives 🏵				
Tasks	**Lessons**	**Pages**	**Exercises**	**Pages**
Customizing Paragraphs				
Control Pagination	Lesson 1.1 Titles 1 to 3	14 to 15	Exercise 1.1 Points 1 to 3	18
Sort paragraphs in lists and tables	Lesson 1.1 Title 4	16	Exercise 1.1 Point 4	18
	Lesson 1.3 Title 1	40	Exercise 1.3 Point 1	58
Formatting documents				
Create and format document sections	Lesson 2.1 Titles 1 and 2	114 and 115	Exercise 2.1 Points 1 and 2	116
Create and apply character and paragraph styles	Lesson 1.2 Titles 1 to 3	22 to 28	Exercise 1.2 Points 1 to 3	34
Create and update document indexes and tables of contents, figures, and authorities	Lesson 2.3 Titles 4 to 9	140 to 149	Exercise 2.3 Points 4 to 9	154 to 156
Create cross-references	Lesson 2.2 Title 7	127	Exercise 2.2 Point 7	130
Add and revise endnotes and footnotes	Lesson 2.2 Titles 1, 3, 4	120, 124	Exercise 2.2 Points 1, 3, 4	129 and 130
Create and manage master documents and subdocuments	Lesson 2.4 Titles 1 and 2	164	Exercise 2.4 Points 1 and 2	167
Move within documents	Lesson 2.2 Titles 5 and 6	125 and 126	Exercise 2.2 Points 5 and 6	130
Create and modify forms using various form controls	Lesson 3.1 Titles 1 to 5	172 to 175	Exercise 3.1 Points 1 to 5	178 and 179
Create forms and prepare forms for distribution	Lesson 3.1 Titles 6 and 7	176 and 177	Exercise 3.1 Points 6 and 7	180

Tasks	Lessons	Pages	Exercises	Pages
Customizing Tables				
Use Excel data in tables	Lesson 1.3 Titles 7 to 9	49 to 55	Exercise 1.3 Points 7 to 9	59 and 60
Perform calculations in Word tables	Lesson 1.3 Titles 3 and 4	45	Exercise 1.3 Points 3 and 4	58
Creating and Modifying Graphics				
Create, modify, and position graphics	Lesson 1.5 Titles 1 to 6, 8, 9, 11, 12, 14 to 17	80 to 95, 97 to 101	Exercise 1.5 Points 1 to 6, 8, 9, 11, 12, 14 to 17	103 to 106
Create and modify charts using data from other applications	Lesson 1.4 Titles 1 and 2	66 to 71	Exercise 1.4 Points 1 and 2	75 and 76
Align text and graphics	Lesson 1.5 Title 10	96	Exercise 1.5 Point 10	105
Customizing Word				
Create, edit, and run macros	Lesson 4.1 Titles 1 to 3	218 to 220	Exercise 4.1 Points 1 to 3	224
Customize menus and toolbars	Lesson 4.2 Titles 1 to 3	228 to 231	Exercise 4.2 Points 1 to 3	234
Workgroup Collaboration				
Track, accept, and reject changes to documents	Lesson 4.4 Titles 1 and 2	246 and 250	Exercise 4.4 Points 1 and 2	267
Merge input from several reviewers	Lesson 4.4 Titles 1 and 2	247 and 254	Exercise 4.4 Points 1 and 2	267
Insert and modify hyperlinks to other documents and web pages	Lesson 4.5 Title 5	278	Exercise 4.5 Point 5	282
Create and edit Web documents in Word	Lesson 4.5 Titles 1 to 3	276 to 277	Exercise 4.5 Points 1 to 3	281
Create document versions	Lesson 4.4 Titles 5 and 6	258	Exercise 4.4 Points 5 and 6	268

TABLE OF OBJECTIVES

Tasks	Lessons	Pages	Exercises	Pages
Protect documents	Lesson 4.4 Titles 3 and 4	255 to 257	Exercise 4.4 Points 3 and 4	268
Define and modify default file locations for workgroup templates	Lesson 4.4 Title 7	260	Exercise 4.4 Point 7	268
Attach digital signatures to documents	Lesson 4.4 Title 8	262	Exercise 4.4 Point 8	268
Using Mail Merge				
Merge letters with a Word, Excel, or Access data source	Lesson 3.2 Title 1	185	Exercise 3.2 Point 1	205
Merge labels with a Word, Excel, or Access data source	Lesson 3.2 Title 7	201	Exercise 3.2 Point 7	207
Use Outlook data as mail merge data source	Lesson 3.2 Title 1	185	Exercise 3.2 Point 1	205

A

AUTHENTICATION

B

BOOKMARK

BREAK

C

CALCULATION

CAPTION

CHART

CHECK BOX

CITATION

CLIP ART

CLIP ORGANIZER

COLOUR

COLUMN

CONDITION

COPYING

CROSS REFERENCE

INDEX

D

DATA FORM

See RECORD

DATA SOURCE

See MAIL MERGE

DATASHEET

DELETING

DIGITAL SIGNATURE

DISPLAY

DOCUMENT

DOCUMENT MAP

DRAWING

See also OBJECT

DROPDOWN LIST

See FORM

E

EMBEDDING

ENDNOTE

See NOTE

F

FIELD

See also FORM, MAIL MERGE

FIELD CODE

See also FORM

O

P

R

INDEX

INDEX

List of available titles in
the Microsoft Office User Specialist collection

Visit our Internet site for the list of the latest titles published.
http://www.eni-publishing.com

ACCESS 2002
ACCESS 2000
EXCEL 2000 CORE
EXCEL 2000 EXPERT
EXCEL 2002 CORE
EXCEL 2002 EXPERT
OUTLOOK 2000
OUTLOOK 2002
POWERPOINT 2000
POWERPOINT 2002
WORD 2000 CORE
WORD 2000 EXPERT
WORD 2002 CORE
WORD 2002 EXPERT

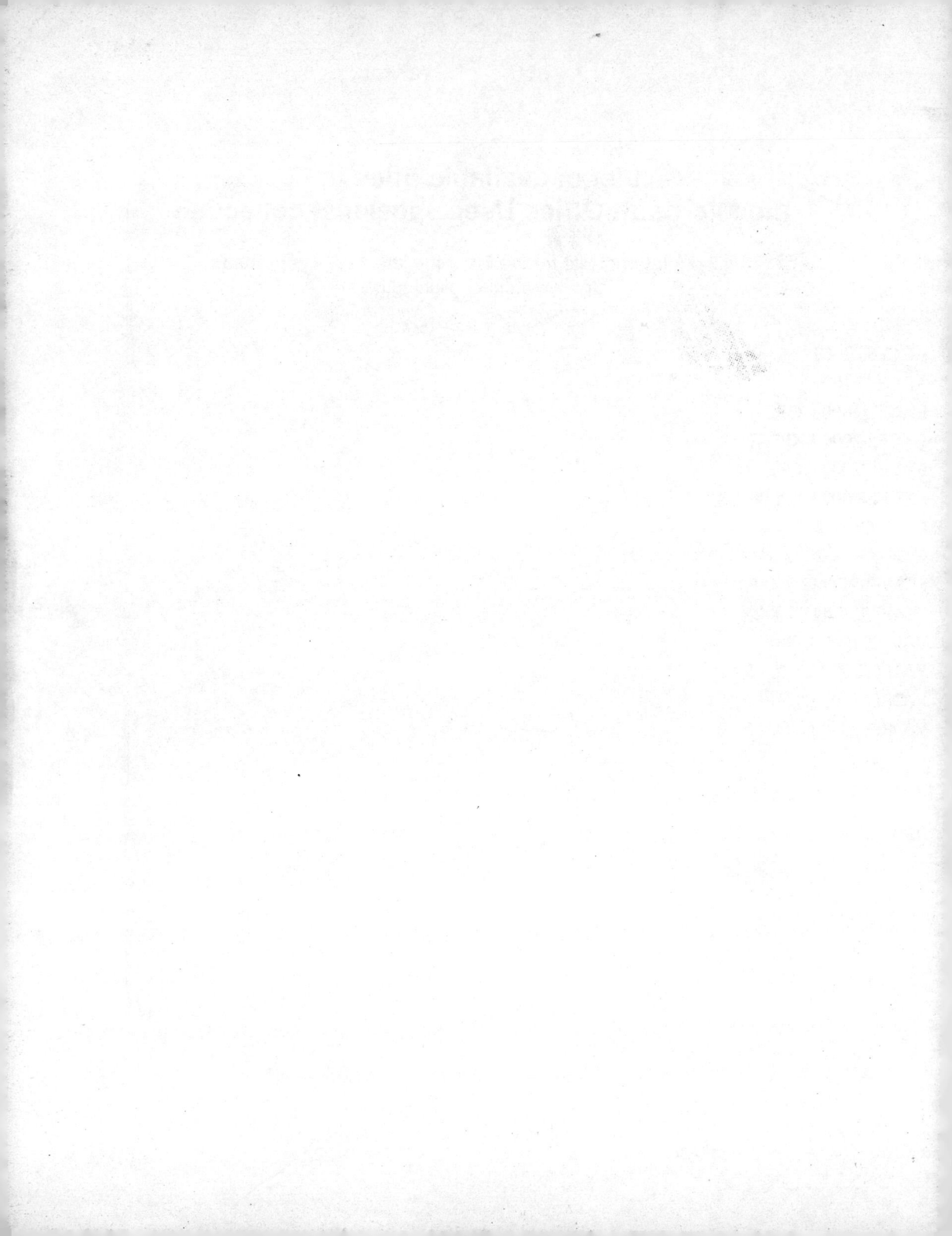